Borrowing for Your Business
Winning the Battle
for the Banker's "Yes"

Borrowing for Your Business
Winning the Battle
for the Banker's "Yes"

George M. Dawson

WITHDRAWN

Upstart Publishing Co., Inc. • Dover, NH 03820

Borrowing for Your Business
Winning the Battle for the Banker's "Yes"
by George M. Dawson

Copyright © 1991 by George M. Dawson
Published by Upstart Publishing Company, Inc.

   Publishers of Independent Business Management Tools
   12 Portland Street, Dover, New Hampshire 03820
   (800) 235-8866 or (603) 749-5071

Printed in the U.S.A.

Library of Congress Card Catalog Number: 91-065C78

ISBN: 0-936894-30-X

Acknowledgments

A number of people were kind enough to read draft copies of this book. I would particularly like to thank the following for their time, their suggestions, and their encouragement. Keith LaRose (Baton Rouge, LA), John Potter (San Antonio, TX), Ron Turner (San Antonio, TX), Edythe Miller (Sherman Oaks, CA), Jan Norman (Santa Ana, CA), Catherine Hesness (Madison, WI), David Bowen (San Antonio, TX), Robert Harris (Aspen, CO), an anonymous banker (Cleveland, OH), John Tallent (Houston, TX), Professor Ed Lodell (San Antonio, TX), Steve LeFever (Seattle, WA), and Pat Morgan (San Antonio, TX). And a special thanks to Eunice Payne of Tuscaloosa, Alabama for her time and expert advice.

Table of Contents

Introduction

I was asked why I decided to write this book. It more or less just happened as an extension of my personal interests and business career.

America seems to have recently reinvented or rediscovered the smaller business enterprise. But the owner-managed business (I dislike the term entrepreneur) never really went away. It has always been here. Small business arrived with the Mayflower.

In the 1960s, when I was in graduate school, giant corporate America was in the spotlight. Students at the Harvard Business School, responding to the lack of regular courses on smaller businesses, formed an extracurricular organization in which I took part called the Small Business Club.

My first assignment after completing my training at a Midwestern bank was to a loan division that dealt primarily with high-income corporate executives, lawyers, accountants, and medical professionals. A few business owners from the neighboring downtown area ended up by default in the division. These businesses were not considered large enough or important enough to ascend the escalator to the Corporate Loan Division. Within our division these local businesses were usually assigned to either the newest officer (me) or to one particular officer (Ken) nearing the end of his career.

I always considered this rather curious, because these business owners were a lot more interesting and certainly less inclined to prima donna behavior than our other customers. Looking back, nearly thirty years later, I realize how fortunate I was to have Ken as a coach, teacher, and role model.

After several years, I was promoted to the "Big Time," national accounts lending, and assigned to work with some of the largest companies in America, the Fortune 500. But it became a drag spending a third of my days traveling to corporate home offices located anywhere east of the Mississippi River. And these companies weren't as interesting to me as the local downtown businesses. With these giant companies my role was pretty much reduced to responding to the business equivalent of commands such as "heel" and "fetch." But it was great being out of the office, independent, and on my own for days at a time.

After some more time I was offered a transfer from the life of a corporate road warrior to the ivory towers of research, planning, economics, marketing, and product management. Fast forward through some stimulating years and some dreadful Wisconsin winters and I was again home in Texas, where I joined a major bank group and was responsible for developing products and new business acquisition programs aimed at the "smaller" large corporation. This was called the Middle Market—i.e., the businesses that don't quite make it onto *Fortune* magazine's list of the top 1,000 companies in America.

Except that there weren't an awful lot of these Middle Market businesses around in the six or so cities where we had banks. So we had to go after the owner-managed community business as well. The work was fascinating. I did research, got a business newsletter underway, launched a series of financial management seminars for business owners, developed sales training and customer contact programs for bank loan officers, and created new brochures and sales campaigns. I ran around training the bank officers in selling, operated financial management seminars for customers in five cities, and taught loan and credit analysis at night to bankers.

After a while I could not stand to run up and down the sidelines any more and I asked to be transferred to a lending division. Lady Luck smiled. There was an opening in the group that made the most interesting kinds of loans—asset-based—to the most interesting kinds of companies—locally owned and managed—and Houston was sliding into a recession.

Because of the recession, the asset lending group needed to place more attention on the borrowers we already had. Were the businesses really well run? Would they survive? Was the collateral pledged to our loans sufficient? Were the borrowers' financial statements accurate and reliable?

And I got to do all of that! I spent most of my time out of the bank at our borrowers' businesses: oil pipe companies, furriers, hardware distributors, truck riggers, forging manufacturers, men's clothing stores, wholesalers of safety equipment or plumbing supplies, and two dozen more; digging around, learning the business, counting and tracking and getting to know these real live businesspeople very well. In fact too well for some of them, as we shut down their companies.

I learned very quickly what the business owner thought about banks and the borrowing experience. I saw how little they understood about how bank borrowing really works or doesn't work and how this gives the banker an edge.

Things change. Banks merge. People make mistakes. Several years later I resigned from heading a professional and executive loan department at yet another bank. Bored with my lawyer-accountant-medical customers, anchored to my office with committees and administrative duties, and missing the real live people of the daily business world, I wanted out.

For the past five years I have worked for South Texas-based owner-managed companies—printers, medical laboratories, plant rentals, air conditioning contractor, tile setters, etc.—as a financial consultant, preparing loan packages, building financial models, and negotiating with my clients' banks and trade creditors. I have a good understanding of how both sides of the borrowing process work and what the major issues are going to be.

Recently, I met the business editor of a major local newspaper. We started talking. The conversation became an article. The article became six more. The newspaper articles became a national magazine article. So this book happened. It is what I do. It is what I tell my clients. It is the framework I bring to each borrowing request. It seemed like a good idea at the time I started to write. It seems like a good idea now that I am done. I hope you think so too.

George M. Dawson
P.O. Box 791283
San Antonio, TX 78279
1991

---

* I plan to use the pronouns *he* and *she* alternately throughout this book. This style may be a little confusing at first, but you'll quickly get used to it.

Chapter 1
Winning the Battle
for the Banker's "Yes"

This is a book for business owners and about bankers: it is for borrowers and about lenders.

It is written for the owner-managed business: those companies where one person or a very few people do it all, manage it all, run the risks, and get the rewards. These companies rarely have a full-time financial officer or financial adviser. They have an internal bookkeeper and an outside accountant who prepares the tax return.

When the company is growing or equipment needs replacement or the business experiences seasonal patterns or profits sag, it borrows money reluctantly from outsiders, including commercial finance companies and factors. For the most part, however, they borrow from lenders of depositors' money, such as banks, savings and loans, and credit unions. Commercial banks provide close to 90 percent of small business short-term loans and about 70 percent of long-term small business loans.

Even when these companies are successful borrowers, they feel unappreciated by their banks. They are frustrated by an atmosphere, procedures, and attitudes in a process they don't understand or control.

The borrowing experience is unbalanced. The borrower deals with lenders only infrequently and usually in a time of need and under deadline pressures. The lender deals all the time with borrowers and conducts business in an organization that formally schedules the decision making process through a "loan committee."

There are training courses for lenders. There are no training courses for borrowers. There are distinguished and rigorous schools for bankers, but there is only the school of experience for borrowers.

The lenders have data bases, trade journals, industry associations, and even conventions. The borrowers are not at all organized. If it existed, wouldn't the National Association of Borrowers have a whale of a convention?

Borrowers risk not knowing how to present themselves to their best advantage in a game they play infrequently. They often take what they can get and don't get what they need.

Some individual bankers are poorly trained and not even remotely qualified to evaluate business credit. Borrowers need to know how to protect themselves against a dangerous and indifferent loan officer who is dealing from a position of power.

The borrowing experience can have many unpleasant results including wasted time, too much money lent, mismatching of need and repayment schedules, or the panicky snuffing out of a business by collateral foreclosure.

This book shows the practical, get-it-done business owner how to deal with the judgmental, bureaucratic, administrative process of lending depositors' money.

To get a loan you must separate yourself from all the hopeful borrowers who look like losers to the bank. You must excite the loan officer. You must stand out from the crowd. You want the loan officer to know that you are different from the "typical" unprofessional and unprepared businessperson.

Business books and government publications offer excellent outlines for preparing business plans or loan requests. However, a mechanical fill-in-the-blanks approach to these outlines doesn't necessarily bring success. Getting a loan is like making a sale. You cannot make a sale if you do not understand the buyer's needs, motivation, and limits.

Successful business borrowers know how best to handle the lender's hidden agenda of questions and check points. They select the proper bank (Chapter 2) and the proper loan officer (Chapter 3), and they understand the pressures on the bank (Chapter 4) and on the loan officer (Chapter 5).

Successful borrowers arrive at a meeting with the banker well prepared, confident, and enthusiastic. They are able to lower the level of risk presented to the bank (Chapter 6) and to anticipate the lender's questions and concerns (Chapter 7).

The bank will always ask seven questions in any borrowing situation (Chapter 8). It doesn't matter if this is your first or your fiftieth loan. These questions might not be asked directly, but they are in the front of the banker's thoughts.

Until you have the answers to these seven questions, don't even think about asking for a loan. If you cannot answer these questions to the banker's satisfaction, you will not get your loan. It is as simple as that.

Many industries have their own special phrases or words that pull together and outline key reminder points. The banking industry is no different. So in addition to the seven logical and objective questions, there are the five C's of credit: Character, Capacity, Conditions, Collateral, and Capital (Chapter 9). These elements can be more subjective than the questions, but are equally essential to making the credit decision.

Banks operate on paper, history, documentation, and records. Bankers are trained to think in particular patterns. So your loan proposal should be well organized and in a format (Chapter 10) that makes analysis and processing easy.

Lending is not cut and dried. Although each borrower presents somewhat different dimensions, banks often approach them as if "one size fits all." It is the borrower's responsibility (Chapter 11) to negotiate terms and conditions that are a good fit for their business.

Nothing is forever. Many loans are structured to require a renewal. Borrowers often fail to manage the bank relationship after the initial loan (Chapter 12) and create unnecessary difficulties for themselves at renewal time.

Loans for small amounts and Small Business Administration (SBA) loans are troublesome. Dealing with a failing bank, handling a loan turndown, or not being able to pay as you agreed are special situations discussed in Chapter 13.

Talking the buyer's language always helps make the sale. There are some special analytical tools and techniques (Special Appendix) that banks use. The winning borrower understands and uses them also. In the

final analysis the businessman is responsible for the borrowing relationship and the banker is responsible for the lending relationship. The
banker may be friendly, but he or she is not your friend. Borrowing from
a caretaker of deposits is a competitive situation in which both sides can
try for a win-win conclusion.

Chapter 2
Selecting Your Bank

Selecting a bank for your business is not an easy process. All banks are not alike. Savings and loans are not banks, even though they sometimes try to act like banks. All savings and loans are not alike either.

I spent several years working with bank advertising. For some reason, at least back then, people believed bank advertising. Understand that those who write the ads are not the folks responsible for the quality of service you receive or for the decisions made about your loan. Bank advertising to local businesses promotes the bank the way bank management thinks its customers see it. It is a poor guide to bank selection.

Certainly you want to stay away from banks that are weak and in trouble. You want a bank that is profitable and growing in capital base and loan totals.

Your local newspaper's business section should tip you off about the strength and safety ratings of your local banks. There are information services (Veribanc 1-800-442-2657 and Sheshunoff 1-512- 472-2244) that will sell you bank ratings. The local business grapevine usually knows the weaker banks.

The law requires the bank itself to provide you with a financial disclosure statement. Using this statement, divide total capital by total assets, and if you get less than six percent the bank is undercapitalized. Net profits after taxes divided by total assets should be close to one percent or better. Ask the bank if it is under "direct regulatory operating supervision." A yes answer means the bank is in serious trouble and is really being run on a day-to-day basis by a government supervisor.

Banks are regulated by the government supervisors for the safety of the small depositor. The small depositor has less than $100,000 in the bank in one or more of several permitted styles of deposit ownership. No government regulator looks out for the business borrower.

If you are sure your business will never need to borrow money, then concentrate on selecting a convenient bank. Look for quality and reliability in the non-borrowing services your business needs. These services could include wire transfer payments, check reconciliation service, payroll deposit, or other transaction and processing services.

It is hard to check these services out ahead of signing on. You can ask the bank for references to other customers and then check it out. If the bank should let you down afterward, you can move on to another bank. It might be an inconvenience, but it can usually be done. Even if you are a non-borrower, always have a backup bank where you at least keep a checking account and know some of the loan officers.

For borrowers, a backup bank is a necessity. A bank's willingness and ability to lend can change with new management, with new ownership, with changes in the bank's financial health, and with local economic or industrial activity.

If you are a borrower and your bank is in difficulty with the regulators, you should move your loan to an untroubled bank without delay. There is more detail on this in Chapter 13.

Let's assume that you know your company will need to borrow money in a matter of a few months. How do you go about selecting the right bank to approach?

Be very careful about the bank that has the reputation of being an easy touch. A newly opened bank might want to build up its loan totals. A formerly sleepy, conservative bank under aggressive new management might be stretching for loan growth. A bank might be just learning how to lend in a new industry—like the Yankee banks lending into the Texas Oil Patch—and be willing to take on any kind of risky deal.

Why should you care about these kinds of things if you get the money you want? Because banks can blow hot and cold in their willingness to make loans. Today's aggressive loan can be tomorrow's mistake. Attitudes change with new management or with experience. Perceived levels of loan risk change as industries move through economic cycles and fall in and out of favor with lenders.

Banks are all different, and those differences show up in the kinds of loans they make and with whom they do business. There are cotton banks and tobacco banks and military banks and consumer banks and banks for rich people and banks that lend only within a five-mile radius of their office and on and on.

If there is a bank that has developed a special reputation and expertise in your industry, it should be at the top of your list. A smart company tries to build a borrowing relationship, not just get a loan from any bank.

Do not pick a bank that is too small to handle your loans. All banks have a legal lending limit: the maximum amount the regulators allow that bank to lend to any one borrower. It does not matter how strong the borrower's financial position is. This ceiling changes from time to time, and it is different for national banks and for state banks.

If you want to bother to figure out the legal limit, the common rule is 10 to 15 percent of the sum of the bank's capital, surplus, undivided profits, and reserve for loan losses. You can find these numbers in the bank's most recent "Statement of Conditions," which you can get from the bank's Cashier. It is a lot easier and more accurate to ask the Cashier about the bank's legal limit. The banks where I worked always had their own lower "house maximum" amount that could be lent to any one borrower. It tended to be around 75 percent of the regulated legal limit.

This legal limit concern is not a minor technicality. I know a growing company whose available collateral would have permitted loans larger than their bank's legal limit. The company needed the additional borrowings, but the bank's legal limit would not allow them to lend any more money. At that time both the general economy and the borrower's industry conditions were tough. The other banks in town did not want to take on my client as a new borrower and bail out the lending bank. The borrower made it through the cash squeeze, but only because of generous extensive credit from his suppliers.

As you want to have some reserve borrowing power for your company, so you want your bank to have some reserve lending power. I would suggest that you double the maximum amount you think your company will need to borrow in the reasonable future. Then look only at banks with a legal limit able to handle that amount.

Next consider a locally owned organization and probably a bank not part of a large bank holding company. The holding companies have publicly traded stock listed on major stock exchanges. These holding companies will tell you that they bring the best of all worlds to their customers; they have not only the sophistication and clout of a major banking organization but also the hometown touch.

It is a rare bank holding company where the management has a significant ownership position in the company stock. Hired professional managers make the decisions and they base them on what is best for the whole organization, not on what is best for your town or for the holding company bank in your town. These professional managers will become wealthy only if they can exercise management stock options and have the price of the company stock increase in value. Their salaries will also increase as the holding company becomes larger and they have more to manage. The holding company grows by buying out independent banks with holding company stock. The more the stock is worth, the fewer shares are needed to buy more banks.

There is nothing wrong with this, except that it can put pressure on the holding company management to make short-term decisions, decisions that have a favorable impact on reported earnings and on the price of the company's common stock. Time also gets spent on fancy annual reports, communicating with the Wall Street stock analysts and brokerage firms, and unfortunately, in some cases, following financial fads and "looking good."

Your local holding company bank manager or loan officer, who may be transferred to another location, is rewarded for following company policies. Policies that may be short-term, variable, and not responsive to your community needs. You in turn are rarely dealing with the final decision maker. This may never cause a problem for your company, but do you want to run the risk that it might?

Smaller businesses are often unable to get the attention they want in a larger bank and to move past dealing with junior, less experienced officers. You need to distinguish yourself from the run-of-the-mill customer and to penetrate this indifference. However, no bank large or small, holding company or independent, has to care about your business loan needs.

A bank's apparent position of strength is not always a reality. A bank is not necessarily expert in lending to business in general or to your type of business in particular. I am reminded of a suburban bank whose lending officers were untrained to read financial statements. They were more knowledgeable in car loans than business loans. Holding company management pressured them to chase new business loans. They did and the bank took heavy loan losses the following year.

A locally owned bank with local businessmen on its board of directors is more likely to be in tune with the needs of community businesses and to take a longer-term view of loan policies. They can be more flexible within limits, but local banks are seen by the same regulators that see the big banks.

You run the risk of less privacy as a small bank borrower. If the management of the bank is also its major owner, you risk having some arbitrary personal credit preferences and prejudices influence loan policies.

Bank ownership is on record with your state's Department of Banking for state banks and the Comptroller of the Currency in Washington, D.C., for national banks. A bank's organizers, the majority shareholder, and all shareholders of publicly held banks should be available public information. Ask around and find out who owns the bank and what else they own. Are they out-of-town, semi-professional financial types? At one time in the Midwest it was profitable to buy a small bank, drive up the earnings, and then sell out to a holding company. Are they shady local wheelers and dealers in debt up to their eyeballs? Look for ownership by solid local people with other business interests and deep pockets.

My personal preference is to have the smaller local bank as the primary lending bank and the larger holding company as the backup.

Nothing is perfect, however, and much is determined by personalities. The local bank still might not be the best place. Get a financial statement of the bank and look at the board of directors. Do you know who they are? Are they the kind of people you would like to know? Would you be comfortable talking to them? Do the directors seem to be people who would be in touch with the reality of doing business in your town? Are any of them your customers or your suppliers or your competitors? Does it matter if these folks learn about your business finances? Look at the ages of the people in the bank, especially management and the senior loan officers. Are they vigorous people? Are several generations represented and can you relate to them? Do you know any of them socially?

Make sure your bank has the expertise you need in non-loan commercial transactions such as credit reports on new customers or letters of credit for export and import. If not, can they hook you up with some other source for these services?

When selecting a bank certainly think geographically for convenience, but also look for a bank with a reputation of serving your industry or your customers or your suppliers particularly well.

Ask other business owners, your key suppliers, and your major customers which banks they use and why. Ask about banks at your local Kiwanis or Rotary meetings. Pay particular attention to any bank officers that are named.

Look at the checks your customers give you and see which banks they use. If you bank where your major customers bank, you can deposit and collect on their checks the same day. Look at the endorsement on the checks you paid to your suppliers. That will tell you where they deposit. It may not be where they borrow, but is there a pattern that points to a particular bank or banks?

Assure whoever discusses a bank with you that you will not approach the bank and use their name without permission. Someone may offer to introduce you to their bank. Beg off on their help until you are fully ready. You don't want to embarrass an important trade relationship with a poor first impression at their bank. Also, the stronger your sponsor, the better you look, so be selective. You want to control the timing and the approach to your potential bank. A bank is a highly structured organization, but it is made up of individuals. That is important to remember, because the right banker is even more critical to your business than the right bank.

Chapter 3
Selecting Your Banker

The selection of a bank and of a banker are almost inseparable activities. When I started in banking, the professional banker enjoyed a wonderful image in the community. In fact, banks severely underpaid their people knowing that the prestige of the job would attract and retain employees. Titles, desks, and carpets substituted for pay raises.

In 1989 the banking industry's image hit its lowest point since the Great Depression. The leaders of many banks were unable to steer their organizations through the economic storms of the past ten years, and that was big news. However, many smaller community-based banking organizations continued to do well. From my perspective the reality has always been that less than 20 percent of the people employed in any particular job ever excel at what they do. The remaining 80 percent range from average to incompetent. This is true in all walks of life from waiters to consultants to bankers.

When you as a businessperson approach a loan officer, the chances are no better than two in ten that you are going to meet one of the truly capable lenders. In a 1990 article the president of the banking industry's major association of credit officers stated that 70 percent of all commercial lenders have fewer than three years' experience in lending.

Furthermore, the best loan officers graduate from the small business loan department to deal with bigger borrowers. It takes almost as much time, if not more, to make a $10,000 loan as it does a $100,000 loan. The bank wants to use its best loan officers efficiently and protect against the larger risks. You don't send your big game hunters out to stalk mice.

There is not much you can do about this. Prepare to deal with a personality that may be passive while you are active; a personality that may be judgmental while you are creative; a person who may be conservative while you are aggressive; a person trained to look at the negative when you are looking at the positive.

Don't be surprised if you feel you are more ambitious, brighter, and will make more money than your banker. You may be correct.

In your conversations with other business people, customers, and suppliers, ask them to rate their bankers for you. In the best of worlds, you will hear good reports about a senior level officer at a financially strong and locally owned bank. You will hear both negative and positive comments about individual local bankers. One negative report on an individual shouldn't knock him or her off your list of potential bankers; there are always two sides to every story. Several negative reports on the same individual, however, should be taken seriously.

You may also receive glowing reports about the wonderful, friendly, easygoing banker who makes borrowing so easy. He never asks a lot of questions, and does everything on a ninety-day note with very little paperwork.

Borrowing can be too easy. Companies can be "over lent" by their banker and get deeper into trouble. There are times when the best loan is no loan. Overly generous lenders are a danger both to their customers and to their bank. The customer depends on repeated bail-out loans and never learns to operate profitably or to curb excessive growth. Each additional loan pyramids an already unstable situation. Eventually it will stop, usually with losses to both the customer and the bank.

Ideally your first visit with a banker should be by appointment and through a referral from one of his solid customers. This doesn't happen a lot, but it is very valuable if you can manage it. Bankers are trained to be suspicious of strangers. The world is full of con men who know where the money is kept. Know your customer or borrower is one of the first rules of banking. Bankers can be a little paranoid until they get to know you better.

With or without a referral, there is information you want to hear from any loan officer. Ask about his or her career. How many banks has he been with and for how long? Some officers change banks like shirts, moving on every few years. Often they are not skilled lenders and are trying to stay a jump ahead of a poor lending record.

This lender may skip on and leave you in a messy position at the bank. Even though you may be a satisfactory credit risk, there will be the tendency to treat you like one of your former officer's high-risk customers.

Learn whether the officer's experience includes a period of economic recession. Has this person helped borrowers work through tough times? Has this person foreclosed on businesses and seen the impact on people's lives? Is this person likely to panic or get discouraged if the going gets tough? Can you trust his judgment? You want a lender with a balance of experience and technical capability. One of my unhappy friends says he has neckties older than his loan officer.

Ask about the officer's lending authority. How big a loan can he make on his own without asking someone with higher authority to bless it? If his loan authority is less than what you need to borrow, then you will be facing delays waiting for his boss or the loan committee to meet. Ask how long you should expect the bank to take in responding to a loan request.

Ask who sits on the loan committee. How often does it meet? What size loans must be approved by them? Ask whether your loans and deposits will make you a small, average, or larger customer of the bank. Get a sense of how important a customer you might be to the bank.

Can the banker explain banking policies and services so you can understand them? What kinds of loans does the bank not like and why? How are the service charges on your checking account calculated? Does the bank have any areas of special expertise or services that will be particularly helpful for your business?

Most of domestic banking is not very complex. If your banker cannot explain her business to you, then how can you trust her to explain your business to her boss or to a loan committee? A small business borrower needs a loan officer who is an effective representative. Try to learn how much stroke your loan officer really has in the bank.

Don't expect the lender at a smaller bank to know a lot about your business. Ask whether others from your industry—your customers, suppliers, and competitors—use the bank.

Are there any types of loans or businesses that the loan officer prefers or would like to avoid? Ask how accounts are assigned to officers in the bank. I liked dealing with wholesalers and distributors and wouldn't touch a restaurant if I could help it.

Very large banks have specialized lending departments. There are people who know all there is to know about the beef industry or auto manufacturing or any number of different industries. It is useful if the banker has experience with other companies like yours. However, the person who acts like he knows it all, probably doesn't.

You are a business, not an industry. In many ways your business reflects your individual personality and skills. It is as unique as you are.

The banker should understand how you fit into the local business scene. Does the banker seem interested and excited about having you as a customer? Does she ask good, insightful questions about your business, your customers, the competition, and pay attention to your answers? You want someone who is interested in learning how your business works and what is important to your success. You need to decide if you can count on this banker to respond to your needs and to effectively represent your interests. If you cannot develop rapport with the loan officer, if he seems disinterested, avoids direct answers, talks a lot about the loan committee and the regulators, or if you just don't feel comfortable with this person, then write this banker off and move on.

One of my first bosses recognized "chemistry." Some people just get along better together than others. If we felt that we couldn't establish a good understanding with a borrower, it was okay to ask that another officer be assigned to that loan.

You have the same right as a borrower. If the chemistry is not right, ask to be assigned another officer. The bank won't like it, and it may prove awkward at first, however, there is no reward in tolerating an unsatisfactory relationship as important as borrowing for your business. Also if your loan officer is a jerk, guess who else knows it? If you still think this is the bank for you, ask to visit with the loan officer's boss as well or other officers who might be handling your account.

There are some really fine business loan officers—I have known several—but the reality is that you may have to deal with a less than satisfactory loan officer. Furthermore, you will have to invest time and effort into getting this officer up to speed and in building a good relationship with the bank.

Chapter 4
Pressures on Banks

The economic role of banks in society is technically defined as a financial intermediary. They link those who have money—depositors—with those who need money—borrowers. Banks are part of a distribution system, gathering and packaging deposits and reselling these deposits as loans. Banks are also part of the payment system. They move money from one depositor to another with checks, drafts, and wire transfers. Most of all, banks are safekeeping warehouses for depositors' money. This role is so important that the government taxes the banks to set up a deposit insurance fund run by the Federal Deposit Insurance Corporation.

For many years government regulators gave banks protected market territories and then controlled interest rates to guarantee profitability. Only the terminally stupid, the incredibly unlucky, or the dishonest bank failed. The regulators didn't have to work very hard either.

Bank borrowers, mainly individual borrowers, have some protection under interest usury laws and non-discrimination laws. All borrowers have some rights under state laws on the enforcement of debts, judgments, seizure and foreclosure of collateral, and so on. The successful expansion of borrowers' rights in the courts has been a difficult matter for the banks.

Bank owners or shareholders receive no special consideration, but in the past had a low risk investment that usually paid a very dependable dividend.

Banks are watched over by both federal and state regulators. Teams of inspectors or examiners visit each bank regularly to make sure the banks are being run for the safety of the depositors; that non-business borrowers are not discriminated against; that the bank is a good citizen of its community; that all banking laws and regulations are observed; and that sound banking practices are correctly followed.

This approach worked well until the 1980s. Then, for several reasons, but basically the failure of banks and the regulators to install and enforce sound lending practices, the system wobbled badly.

Look at a bank's financial setup: Typically, for every dollar of stockholder investments, the bank has ten to twenty dollars of depositors' money. Since the depositors' money must be returned to them, it is a form of debt. Your conservative banker carries a debt-to-worth ratio five to ten times higher than they want to see for your company. To make money the bank lends out its depositors' money and charges interest. Lending out half of the deposits is considered conservative. Lending 80 percent is aggressive.

Here is the arithmetic at the extremes. Assume the bank has $100 of deposits and $5 of stockholder's equity (a deposit-to-equity ratio of 20:1). The bank lends out $80 and puts the remaining $25 in cash, investments, and bank buildings. Loan losses are charged against equity, not deposits. If as little as 6.25 percent of their loans do not pay ($5), it will wipe out 100 percent of the equity. Before even half this amount was lost the regulators would take command of the bank. At a 10:1 deposit-to-equity ratio, it would take 12.5 percent loan losses to wipe out $10 of equity. In real life, with bankers and regulators involved, it is more complicated, but banks have little cushion for error. This makes for a lot of pressure, and it makes them very uptight.

The regulators control bank behavior in a number of different ways, one of which is a surprise personal inspection of the bank by a team of examiners. They go through the bank with a fine-tooth comb. The examiners physically inspect documents and collateral, review procedures, test computer systems, review borrowers' files with the loan officer, and can even count the cash on hand. It is not a lot of fun having the examiners camp out in your bank for days at a time.

Besides these on-site inspections, the regulators require banks to submit periodic financial condition reports, to maintain various dollar reserves for possible loan and security losses, and to maintain specific financial performance ratios. Many of these factors are combined into a CAMEL rating (Capital, Assets, Management, Earnings, Liquidity) which rates the financial health of the bank. When bankers think about CAMELs they aren't planning a desert expedition.

The regulators can establish and enforce policies and procedures on specific banks, can have incompetent bankers fired, and bring charges to put dishonest bankers in jail. Besides the pressuring presence of the regulators, juries and judges have not been kind to banks in recent years. Borrowers and depositors have successfully sued banks on several grounds.

Prior to the early 1970s banks could pretty much step in and control a company that was not paying its loan as agreed. Then business borrowers convinced juries that wrongful bank interference actually caused their businesses to fail. These failed borrowers won substantial damages from the banks. Banks have lost suits alleging they acted in bad faith in extending too much credit, in extending too little credit, in cancelling lines of credit, and even in setting checking account service charges.

If a borrower has an extensive history of business litigation, the bank will be cautious. If a borrower is constantly rolling out his lawyer to nitpick the bank, he will be urged to move his business elsewhere. Banks are now looking over one shoulder at the regulators and over the other shoulder at their customers. This makes them reluctant to provide you with business advice and ideas. They are slow to recommend other businesses and professionals to you. They seem to be unnecessarily cautious and hesitant.

If you want advice from your banker, you ask for it in a way that reassures it won't come back to haunt him. In a disagreement, don't threaten the bank unless you mean it. Threats to sue a bank, like bomb jokes in airports, are now taken very seriously.

Banks understand the need for confidentiality with their customers' information, but their own operations are wide open to virtually anyone who wants to look. A bank's financial performance is a matter of public record. Each quarter you can determine the growth, market share and profitability of your local banks from financial statements published in your local newspaper.

Business information services buy computer tapes from the Federal Deposit Insurance Corporation and publish heavyweight books of industry statistics and comparisons. Banks can easily compare their financial structure and performance to that of their competitors and to similar or "peer group" banks all over the country. There is no place to hide.

Companies with more than $100,000 in their accounts are performing their own credit analysis on the banks to see which banks are sound enough to be their bank of deposit. Applications for branches, acquisitions, and relocations provide for public notice, hearings, and challenges by other banks and by community interest groups. In this public spotlight, the industry's often inept relations with the press, complicated by newspaper reporters without financial background, and the appearance of sensational investigative television reporters, causes even more banker's paranoia.

Some of my clients want to know why the banker is so suspicious and treats them like criminals. There was a 205 percent increase in bank losses due to fraud and embezzlement from 1983 to 1987. Cases where the criminal was a bank customer, rather than a bank employee, more than doubled from 1983 to 1988. Further, a majority of bank failures seem to have involved outsider fraud.

The banking industry's response is to interview and investigate the potential borrower more carefully. Bankers spend more time and effort on cross-checking the applicant's background and personal and business references, and on more thoroughly searching public records. The fact that the banker knew your father used to count for something. Not any more.

If you are thinking about relocating your business to a new community, spend some time interviewing and getting to know the local banks before you move. Make sure your present bank will serve as a reference for you. Expect the new bankers to be a little suspicious.

Ask a banker how his world is different today from ten years ago. He will tell you about poor economic conditions, overworked and hostile regulators, litigious customers, antagonistic juries, embarrassing publicity, fraudulent borrowers, unhappy shareholders, an unsympathetic public, apathetic employees, and so forth. Not all banks are facing these plagues to the same degree, but it is no wonder, friends still active in banking tell me it's not fun any more.

The major change in banking in the past generation is simply the loss of a very predictable, stable, and controlled operating environment. The opportunity to make an error has never been greater. The consequences of error have never been more severe.

The pressure is on the banks not only to make good quality new loans, but also to reduce the level of risk already on their books. This also means banks are seeking to shift weaker and apparently troublesome loans out of the bank before they become a real problem. (Chapter 12 discusses planning for your loan renewal.)

Certainly there has been some overreacting and the pendulum will swing back, but until then the business borrower, as unfair as it may seem, must deal with this situation.

Cooperate fully with the banker's information needs. Use your lawyer, but keep him or her in the background. Put your accountant in the foreground. Don't hide your weaknesses. Beat the banker to the punch. Identify and overcome the negatives in your borrowing situation as part of your loan request. Be positive and factual. Demonstrate control of your company. Have a business plan.

Be prepared to answer the Seven Questions (Chapter 8) and to satisfy the Five C's (Chapter 9).

Chapter 5
Pressures on the Banker

Borrowing from the bank is a healthy, adversarial business relationship. As I have said elsewhere: Your banker may be friendly, but he or she is not your friend.

According to an article in the *Journal of Commercial Bank Lending,* "The customer should realize that, generally speaking, they are responsible for protecting their own interests and that the officer's role is to protect the legitimate interests of the institution."

It is helpful in negotiating with anyone to understand the needs and the pressures placed upon him or her. This can help you understand why the banker acts the way he does. You need to understand what kinds of things are really important and non-negotiable to the banker.

So first you need to know about the "Oopsers." Everybody in a bank has a boss or some other authority or monitor looking over his shoulder. Internal to the bank there are the auditors, the loan committee, the credit department, the loan review department, the discount department, and the compliance officer. Executive and senior vice presidents watch vice presidents and assistant vice presidents.

The board of directors watches over the chairman. The board of directors represents the stockholders, but more importantly is liable to be sued by borrowers and shareholders. Directors run the risk of being sent to jail for deliberate mismanagement of the bank. Many years ago it was an honor to be a bank director. Now it is a very hazardous honor and it is difficult to get liability insurance coverage.

Sitting at the top of this system of overview are the state and federal agencies that regulate banks. The structure of these agencies, their overlapping authority, relative staffing levels, and competency of their examining and administrative staffs is more than I want to explain.

The base line is that these regulating agencies exist for the protection of the small depositor: the bank customer with less than $100,000 on deposit. The agencies which insure banks come in contact with borrowers only after they have taken over a failing bank. They want to collect all the weak loans and sell all the healthy loans to another bank. They take a tough attitude toward borrowers. The government does not want to take over banks. The government does not want to pay off on Federal Deposit Insurance when a bank goes broke. The system of protection is aimed at keeping the depositors' money safe. It does this by keeping employees from stealing and by making sure the bank gets its depositors' money back from the investments it purchases and from the loans that it makes.

So if you work for a bank, especially as a loan officer, there are all these people looking over your shoulder saying, "Oops, you did that!! Oops, you lent to that company!! Oops, you raised their credit line," and worst of all, "Oops, that's a non-performing loan."

The loan officer is constantly second-guessed by the system. The credit department helps with the initial loan and credit analysis. The loan must be presented and defended either to the officer's boss or to the loan committee. The loan review department analyzes and assigns a quality grade to the loan after it is made. The audit department makes sure that no one stole the loan proceeds. The discount department makes sure the note, collateral assignments, and other paperwork is all in order.

And then the regulators come in for their required exams and review everyone else's reviews. It is amazing that anything gets done. It is also amazing that the system still does not prevent the loan problems and losses experienced in the past several years.

So if you are a banker, how do you avoid looking foolish and keep your job? How do you protect yourself against the regulators? against uncertainty? against risk? against the "oopsers"?

First of all you follow the rules. Most loan decisions of any significant dollar amount are made by more than one person. In theory this collaborative system, the committee approach, provides for a balanced point of view. It gives the loan officer the benefit of the experience of the other loan officers. It brings objectivity to the decision. In practice this system can work pretty well. Besides shared judgment, this committee system also provides the protection of shared blame. If the loan goes bad and cannot be collected, who gets the blame? It is hard to fire the whole loan committee. However, if somewhere in the entire process, if somewhere in the history of the loan relationship, the loan officer has failed to follow the bank's rules, then blame can be officially pinned on that officer. Failure to follow the rules can put a banker in the unemployment line.

Is your loan officer hung up on the bank's rules? Is he inflexible? Does everything seem to take too long? It is almost certain the answer to all of these is yes, but it is unlikely that you can change it.

Always give yourself lots of lead time when you want something from the bank. Start all major transactions weeks ahead of your due date. If you are always putting pressure on the bank to hurry up and to shortcut the rules and procedures, like the little boy who cried "Wolf" you will wear out your welcome.

The time when you really need help may be the time the bank decides to teach you a lesson.

From a borrower's standpoint, you want to deal as high up in a bank's power structure as you can. You want to deal with someone who has the authority or the internal clout to bend a rule or make an exception to "bank policy" once in a while, for your benefit, and get away with it. It is often easier to ask for forgiveness, than it is to ask for permission.

There is a danger here. A bank officer who regularly bends or breaks rules for a customer is a person breaking his word and violating his employer's trust. You would not want this unreliable person as your employee, why would you want him as a loan officer? And eventually the system catches up with him and with you.

Problems often occur with business checking accounts where regular and substantial overdrafts are permitted. The businessperson begins to depend on these overnight or over-the-weekend loans and writes checks well in advance of making deposits. "Good old Fred at the bank will cover the overdrafts."

But good old Fred has been caught and told to follow the rules, or perhaps he has left the bank. Your payroll or tax payment checks bounce. The bank won't lend you the money to cover the overdrafts because you are a poor businessperson who cannot manage your bank account. You are probably in trouble with the tax man as well.

Following the rules provides the banker with protection from the "oopsers." The next step is to build a fortress of file information about borrowers. Loan officers build large files with projections and forecasts and call reports. They put in financial reporting and tracking systems. They try to know the borrower and the key employees very well. Besides providing protection, this is also good common sense.

So when the oopser comes around and says, "George, why did you make that loan?" I say, "Well, let me show you their financials and their history and let me tell you about the management. Let me get the files and show you the market data and the industry projections." At this point the oopser figures I have things under control and leaves me alone. They go off to oops on someone else.

So as problem loans batter the banking industry, your banker has probably shown an increased interest in your company. This is very logical, self-protective behavior. The bankers have become information addicts. Your banker has a very high need for written information about your company. It is in your best interests to cooperate. You wouldn't like it if one of your vendors withheld necessary supplies; the bankers don't like it done to them either.

Another subtle pressure on the banker is the fear you might completely repay your loan. Why? If you pay off your loan, then the bank has to find another loan to replace it. This means another credit analysis, more work, and a new unproven risk. The perfect loan is one the borrower theoretically could repay by slowing company growth, but does not. This "evergreen credit" is a fully collateralized loan secured by accounts receivable and inventory.

The banker loves the borrower whose business is growing at a steady, controlled pace. The company makes all principal and interest payments on time, but their credit needs keep growing. At some future time the debt will be replaced with new equity or long-term non-bank financing and the cycle can start again.

If you do have plans to refinance your bank debt or bring new equity into your company, talk to your banker about it. Get her suggestions and ideas. Make certain your basic loan arrangements are secure and in place. Don't make the bank think it is losing a valued customer to another bank.

Uncontrolled, extremely rapid growth of a company and its borrowing needs really worries loan officers. Experience, their conservative attitudes, and their training tell them that most business owners are unable to manage rapid growth. Bankers believe that sales and manufacturing get management's attention and worry that approval of customer credit, maintaining profit margins, and careful cash management are neglected. And most of the time the banker is right to be worried.

If you are a very rapidly growing company, don't be disappointed at your banker's uneasiness and low level of enthusiasm. Don't get caught by surprise when the bank cuts off additional increases to your loan. You can get the bank to go along further by persuading its officers you are the exception to the rules. Use cash flow projections to show the bank you understand that a growing company uses cash more rapidly than it can create the cash it needs.

If the bank talks about more equity, finding another lender to share your loan, or long-term financing from a non-bank lender, you are on thin ice. Show your plans, your benchmarks, your controls and answer the endless questions. Try to get a sense of how far the bank will go. If you give the banker the impression you are simply hanging on to a runaway train, he will not wait for the next station to get off.

A major pressure factor hanging over the banker is the Internal Revenue Service. The IRS is like the 600-pound gorilla that can sleep wherever it wants to. The IRS can bulldoze its way through almost anyone. Some businesses treat the payment of employee withholding taxes lightly. These businesspeople believe they can turn the money in late or not at all. They plan to tap dance around the government bureaucracy with late and partial payments and eventually get caught.

Once the IRS starts to move against a borrower that is delinquent in its tax payments, the bank loses control of the situation and can lose its collateral to the IRS. Worse yet, in certain circumstances the bank can become liable for some of the borrower's unpaid taxes.

Nothing puts the chill on your ability to borrow quite like tax trouble. A loan to pay delinquent business taxes is one of the toughest loans to get approved in a bank. You are branded as a poor businessperson. One banker I know refers to companies in tax trouble as zombies, the living dead.

Once you work your way out of the IRS jam, your banker may forgive, but she won't forget. Your risk rating has gone up. She will regularly want you to prove that you are current with taxes.

Besides the matter of not paying what is owed, banks also don't like borrowers lying about their company's income or expenses to the IRS. This is politely called under-reporting income.

How uptight can banks get? Very. A director of a small Houston bank was told to move his company's borrowings and resign his directorship when it was learned he was paying his mother and his daughter high salaries for minimal work. Is that too uptight? I don't know, but it happened.

The bank will ask for both your company tax returns and your company financials. Any differences between your income tax returns and your company financials need to be explained. If the differences are not explainable because of standard accounting practices, an honest banker has no interest in working with your company.

Certain businesses have the reputation of being tied to organized crime. It is difficult, but necessary, for the honest companies in these fields to overcome a bank's initial suspicions.

Lenders look closely for "skimming" in businesses that deal mainly in cash: self-service car washes and laundromats, for example. The banks understand tax minimization through legal means, but won't cooperate with illegal tax evasion.

The very nature of the loan officer's work creates pressures. The loan officer's job has built-in conflict of interest opportunities: accepting gifts and entertainment from customers, profiting from insider information, doing business with customers. What might be normal customer and supplier entertainment practices in your industry could be viewed as excessive and inappropriate with your banker.

Increasingly adversarial customers, attorneys, and juries have made bankers super cautious about what they tell their customers, about business advice they may give, and about recommendations and referrals to other businesses. Banks used to market themselves as business consultants. Now the loan officer is very careful about giving friendly advice and sharing business information. "Officers should consult counsel," now appears very frequently in bank procedure manuals.

Another source of pressure on a banker is the career path within the industry. Traditionally, bankers were promoted or treated like cheeses. You spent some period of time in a position until you were properly "aged or cured." Then you were rotated or promoted up to the next position for more curing, through experience and increased responsibility with larger borrowers and so on. Your importance in the bank was directly related to the size of the accounts you were assigned.

This process was physically visible in the large open bank platform or lending area. As lenders progressed upward in their career paths, their desk locations moved toward the rear of the lending area. The younger, less experienced officers had the front rows closest to the customers.

Times have changed. Rocket careers in banking are now available for younger people. These opportunities are generally with larger banks, what are called Money Center Banks, in special fields of technology, currency trading, international finance, and cash management.

Things have not changed all that much in the more traditional banking function of local business commercial lending. The reward system is directed toward the officer with the larger portfolio of loans. Pressure continues to be applied on loan officers to generate larger volumes of quality loans. If you are a smaller borrowing customer, in many cases your loan officer's ambition makes him want to "graduate" away from you.

Which customer do you think will get the officer's attention? Which borrower will get most of her advice and time? The larger borrower and the borrower with the clear potential to grow, of course. The smaller borrower is often viewed as a necessary evil and clearly not a major career advancer. This doesn't mean there are not some terrific, well-qualified, caring, small business loan officers. There are, and I have had the privilege of working with some of them.

Most of the time business lending is a buyer's market and the borrower is the seller. In your business you understand your customers' buying motives and organize a selling approach superior to your competition's. As a potential borrower you can really help yourself by making the loan officer look good to his or her superiors and by helping the officer be efficient. Simple things help. Clearly identify any material you present. Have your papers neat and legible. Provide historical information on your company. Educate the lender about your industry and your competition. Promptly return her phone calls. Communicate the growth potential of your business. Ask for reactions, suggestions, and advice. Be courteous. Encourage him to talk. Pay attention. Treat the banker as you would any valued customer of yours.

When your loan officer advances toward the back of the platform, will you have to break in a new officer? Probably yes, but if your working relationship has been good and your business has grown or still has potential, perhaps your officer will keep you in her portfolio. The higher in the power structure you can deal, the better it is for you.

In any event, if you have to start over with a new officer you will start with a good reputation and a personal contact higher up in the power structure.

I remember one long time customer who made it a practice to keep in contact with all his former loan officers, even those who went to other banks. His loans always seemed to go more smoothly in loan committee where he was known to a number of officers. Do you wonder why?

Chapter 6
Risk is a Four-Letter Word

The bankers' main concern is that their depositors' money, lent to businesses, is paid back. There are several major classes of risk that worry bankers: country risk, industry risk, and company/credit risk.

Country risk is mainly a problem for the several hundred banks that lend money to foreign nations or to foreign companies. The borrowing country's economy may collapse or the foreign government can restrict the ability of local companies to pay off debt to US banks. There can be sharp changes in the exchange rate of the foreign currency for US dollars or political changes in attitude toward foreign investors and lenders.

United States banks located along our border with Mexico see country risk affecting their American borrowers. Swings in the purchasing power of the peso strongly impact the business done in border cities like Laredo and El Paso.

Industry risk exists because it is possible for entire industries or industry sectors to turn down and drag even reasonably well-managed companies down with them. Recent collapses in the oil industry and real estate took down with them companies directly involved in these industries, and secondary-level subcontractors, and suppliers of equipment. Towns in oil production centers had third-level effects as local merchants, dentists, and others closed down.

Company or credit risk is very specific to a borrower. Even when the economy is healthy and a particular industry is doing well, individual companies fail. The reasons are many and different: poor location, technological change, too-rapid growth, internal theft, ineffective sales management, and so on.

Banks try to control country risk by developing expert knowledge about these areas and by limiting the dollar amount of loans they are willing to make in particular countries. Only a handful of the largest American banks have the staff and the time to become experts in international loans.

Other larger and medium-sized banks have developed experts in particular industries such as construction, trucking, or coal mining. At the same time these banks diversify and spread out their loans over different industries and different companies.

After the nation's largest 500 banks or so, lending is a local or regional game. It is hard for a bank to diversify its loan risk if its local or regional economy is not internally diversified. Banks located in steel mill towns or oil producing regions don't have much choice. These smaller banks can either be over-concentrated in local loans or called unresponsive to the community if they invest in government securities instead of lending locally.

It is entirely possible for a loan request to be turned down because at the moment the bank wants no more loan concentration in the applicant's industry. Your loan is also likely to be denied if a competitor or a company similar to yours is a recent problem loan at your bank. Bad apples can spoil the barrel for a time.

Banks manage company or credit risk by a thorough evaluation of your loan application, through the bank's credit decision process, and by continuing to track the borrower's performance after the loan is made. Industry risk and company risk come together in the lending process in a technique called "comparative analysis." Your company's financial structure and performance is compared to composite statistics of other companies in your industry.

Most of the country's nearly 15,000 commercial banks are not large enough to develop their own industry experts and data base. They rely heavily upon industry statistics compiled and published by one industry source, the *Annual Statement Studies* of Robert Morris Associates (RMA). The *Studies* contain summary balance sheets, income statements, and financial ratios for a sample of companies within specific industry classifications.

In separate publications, *Lending To Different Industries* and the monthly *Journal of Commercial Bank Lending,* RMA provides research and analysis into the operating characteristics and lending risks of a wide variety of borrowers, ranging from wholesale fuel distributors to retail jewelry stores. These studies discuss the typical borrowing needs of the industry, market trends, collateral values, managing the loan, and numerous other credit details.

Besides the RMA information, banks can also refer to financial statistics available from individual industry associations and from trade groups. Comparative statistics are also available through the credit reporting agency Dun & Bradstreet's *Industry Norms and Key Business Ratios,* accounting groups, and other specialized researchers such as Prentice Hall's *Almanac of Business and Industrial Financial Ratios.*

It is best for you to assume that the banker has little detailed knowledge of your industry and knows little about your company if you are a new customer. The successful borrower always takes on the role of educating the loan officer. If you fail to educate, you take the chance the loan officer will overestimate the industry risks involved and underestimate the strengths of your company. These mistakes will not help get your loan approved.

One of my customers said she always assumed her new loan officer had arrived that morning... from Mars. But there is no need to talk down to the officer in this process. You simply take on the role of the informative, helpful, and well-prepared customer who wants to help the bank have a complete credit file. Of course, you might suggest that some members of the loan committee would appreciate the additional background you are providing. It is useful to include some copies of your industry trade magazines if they explain your business, analyze favorable industry trends, and lend credibility to your business plans. Most bankers are generalists, not specialists, and would not see this information as part of their daily activities.

Order the current RMA *Studies* and see how your company measures up to the industry composite. Order the RMA *Lending to Different Industries* study for your type of business and see what will concern the banker about your industry.

A recent issue of the RMA *Journal* described ten frequently seen elements that increase lending risks to contractors. Two of the elements cited were contractors' lack of equipment cost control and poor billing procedure. If you are a contractor, wouldn't it be smart to include in your loan proposal some information on your procedures to control equipment cost and how you get out your draws and billings promptly and accurately?

If you understand the lender's fears and the key elements of the credit decision ahead of time you can prepare a much more effective and successful proposal. Set up your financial statements for the past three years so you can compare them to the RMA numbers. Get your accountant to help you. Identify those ratios and percentages where your company is different from the RMA industry composite. Understand if these are favorable or not so favorable differences. The Appendix covers ratios in more detail.

Figure out why your company is different from the industry composite. Are they bad reasons or good reason? Are your accounts receivable higher than the industry because your collections are sloppy or because you deal with large credit-worthy customers, while most of the others in your industry do a cash business with small clients?

As in any sales presentation, you anticipate the prospect's objections ahead of time and answer them in your presentation. Also, get any comparative statistics available through your industry associations or trade groups. Make the same kind of analysis and response.

It can happen that the RMA data and the industry association data will be different in format and in the actual ratios and percentages. The RMA data is based on a small, unstructured sample picked by member banks from their files and sent to RMA for compilation into the *Studies*. Because these companies have their financial statements in the bank files, it is likely that they are or were bank borrowers. Because of this the RMA data might contain more of the larger companies in your industry. Association surveys can include more companies and a greater size range of companies than RMA, but the financial data is considered less accurate by the banks.

Leave reference to the RMA data out of your proposal, but answer any weaknesses it suggests. The banker will appreciate having your other independent industry data. You will look like a good manager who studies industry trends.

This industry comparison is not just window dressing. It should be a regular part of any company's management activities. The questions— Where are we different? Is it a good or bad difference? How good or how bad is it? Why is it happening? How do we stop it or make more of it happen?—are vital to the survival of a business.

The next chapter covers in more detail the credit analysis process.

Chapter 7
Loan Evaluation:
An Insider's View

The credit department is that mysterious place where the loan officer "sends" your statements for "spreading" and for credit "analysis." Sounds like some strange ritualistic process, performed by high priests and elders. As a loan officer, I never took borrowers back into the credit department. I was afraid they might get hit by paperwads or Frisbees thrown by management trainees seeking relief from the boredom of spreading financial statements. Worse yet they might meet some of the department's permanent residents—senior credit officers, properly famed for their ability to penetrate even the murkiest financial statement, but with personalities described as "not very social."

I was a credit trainee twice, once fresh out of graduate school, then again twenty years later, at my own request, as a staff vice president being retreaded for a special loan assignment. Except for the too-long-delayed introduction of female trainees and some new Frisbee colors, not much had changed in twenty years.

The credit department is where the loan officers-to-be, the trainees, receive their initial lessons in saying "No." Your carefully prepared financial statements are first placed in the hands of a recent college or business school graduate. The trainee assembles a tidy sectioned file or credit folder for each borrower. These files are the central data collection point for all information on a borrower. The bank regulators review these files to determine if the bank is using proper diligence, judgment, and procedure in making loans. A great deal of effort is spent keeping files up to date. They are checked out to credit analysts, loan officers, and loan review officers like library books. In theory the credit department should always know the whereabouts of every file. It doesn't, and credit files get lost from time to time. A missing credit file will paralyze the progress of that customer's loan request.

The file holds commercial credit bureau reports, loan officer memos and call reports, bank and borrower correspondence, deposit and loan balance histories, identification of other banking services used by the borrower and its principal officers, inquiries received about the customer from other lenders and creditors, the results of inquiries made by the bank on the borrower, data about the borrower's industry, the borrower's financial statements, annual reports, publicity releases, newspaper stories, and anything else the bank thinks is relevant.

The trainee "spreads" your financials into the standard analytical format used by your bank, orders credit reports, perhaps checks out collateral values, and does an analysis of the loan request. These activities are frequently referred to as "grunt work."

The bank's format or spreadsheet is pretty much the standard balance sheet and income statement layout. But now all companies' data has the same appearance, the same items appear in the same place and this makes it easier to review and discuss a loan in loan committee. The spreading can be done by entering your financial statements into a computer program or simply transcribing by hand onto a worksheet that is later typed.

Most banks prefer the computer approach. It reduces typing errors, allows the program to automatically calculate the various financial ratios, and keeps the trainees from fraternizing with the typists. These programs were rare ten years ago, but now several vendors market them to banks and the general public. Some banks suffer from the not-invented-here syndrome and create their own in-house programs.

It is interesting, but certainly not essential, to know which program your bank uses. Ask your loan officer. If the program were for sale, you could run your numbers through beforehand.

The point is your financials are spread into a format and most likely by a green kid. In this spreading, asset, liability, and equity items will be sorted into specific categories. Any items on your financials that are not crystal clear and easily categorized will initially be placed into the least favorable or least liquid category. If you have "commissions receivable" in current assets, but don't specify when they will be paid, the commissions will be reclassified as long-term assets. If you have "notes payable" and don't give the maturity date, the notes will be classified as current liabilities due within one year, even if they are not. Your company can end up looking like it can't pay its bills, much less a bank loan.

Perhaps when the spread sheets are later reviewed by a senior person, some questions will be asked and the analysis corrected. And then again, perhaps not. Why run the risk? Provide good footnotes and explanations. It is better to provide too much detail than too little.

There are rites of passage in the credit department. Somewhere along in the process of spreading company financials, the credit trainee will be asked by a senior person (and everyone in the bank is senior to the credit trainees), "Would you make this loan?" After responding positively several times and getting shot down with the weak points in the loans, the trainee learns. It is less humiliating to offer a qualified "No" than an enthusiastic "Yes."

Other than the somewhat negative tone to the procedure, credit department training at most major banks does a good job of converting classroom financial theory into the nitty gritty detail of the real world. It also weeds out some hiring mistakes, but usually it is a personality rather than a mental capacity issue. Very bright, energetic, and impatient people find the credit department difficult.

Smaller banks cannot afford the overhead of credit trainees, so they hire people away from bigger banks. This makes for consistency in the approach to business credit within the banking community. So regardless of the size of your bank, the effort you give to your loan proposal should be the same.

Besides spreading statements and learning from the resident old timers, the credit trainees also have more classroom time. Many years ago loan officers appeared to fall into one of three categories: collateral lenders, character lenders, or income statement lenders. This is no longer true. The route taken today in larger banks is much more comprehensive and adds a new dominant component: cash flow. This analytical approach is taught by several commercial or business credit training programs specifically designed for the banking industry. In these programs the Seven Questions and the Five C's of Chapters 8 and 9 are organized, codified, built into checklists, grids, and decision trees. More importantly, the trainee/loan officer learns how to prepare and analyze a cash flow projection. The trainee, ready to graduate from a large bank's credit department, is well-indoctrinated into "No," number-crunching, and cash flows.

Does this mean that your own loan officer does not make an independent analysis of your loan request? No, it does not. But your loan officer, depending upon how many borrowers are in her portfolio, may leave much of the number analysis to the credit department. The loan officer will spend time learning about your company—the management, competition—and structuring the loan. One way to look at this process is that the credit department works more on the Seven Questions and the loan officer works directly with the borrower on the Five C's .

It will be the loan officer who carries the ball to get your loan approved. Ask and understand, before you ever have to borrow, how loan authority is allocated at your bank. A fairly common approach is to give each loan officer, depending upon rank, experience, size of bank, and type of customer base, an individual dollar limit loan authority and then build up from that point. For example, I was authorized to make unsecured loans up to $150,000 and secured loans up to $250,000 without any one else's permission in the bank. If I got my boss to sign on a loan with me, the limits rose to $300,000 unsecured and $500,000 secured. Loans over these ceiling limits required a presentation to the loan committee.

Some loan officers have been known to turn down a borrower on their own and then say that the loan committee shot them down. This is pretty sleazy, but saves arguments. Knowing ahead of time what size loan must go to committee will cut out this nonsense. Knowing ahead of time will permit you to meet and cultivate your loan officer's boss.

The credit department may also run your loan application through a credit scoring or grading system. This is an approach that first appeared in retail or consumer lending. Imagine that over the years you have made thousands of loans to purchase cars. You have kept excellent records on the borrowers and how they paid. Now you go back and analyze all that history. You can identify the characteristics of borrowers most likely to pay as agreed and of borrowers most likely to skip town. Such characteristics are home ownership, years on the job, years in town, present debt owed, past payment history, and so on. You assign different numerical weights or values to these financial characteristics.

When a new car loan applicant comes into the bank, you can quickly assign these predictive, experience-based values to the items on the application. You "score" the application and reach a quicker and theoretically more reliable decision about making the car loan. Now try to do the same thing with business loans. It is more difficult, subtler, less certain, but is being done today. There are more than forty different scoring systems now in use. The idea, as with the consumer loans, is to make the credit decision process as objective as possible.

Early rating systems were mostly narrative. No point values were established, but loans were assigned final ratings from "excellent" through "acceptable" to "doubtful" and even "loss." Clearly no one makes a new doubtful loan. The rating systems apply to both new loan applications and to loans already on the books. Banks and regulators always want to know the likely loan losses already sitting in the loan portfolio.

An "excellent" company might be described as "in a growing industry where the immediate situation is healthy, the general outlook excellent, and the company's performance is better than the industry averages." A "good" company would be "in an industry where the current and future conditions are stable and the company's performance is at least equal to the industry averages." This is not very sophisticated stuff, but it does move a little bit out of the "gut feel" approach. Note that the comparison of your company's performance to others in your industry is a real and ever-present theme. Ignore it at your own peril.

The next higher level of commercial loan scoring systems identifies and assigns point counts and relative weights to specific borrower characteristics. The characteristics are grouped by categories such as: financial performance, company and management capabilities, credit reputation, prior experience with the borrower, industry outlook, and collateral.

One system can have as few as four categories and another as many as ten. Under one system the best possible score is 21 points, in another it is 36, and in a third 100. Straight financial characteristics, such as balance sheet ratios, or size of earnings relative to principal and interest payments, make up as much as 75 or as little as 44 percent of the final score.

Banks don't agree among themselves about the best system. It's unlikely your bank will show you its scoring system. You can always ask. You should at least ask if the bank uses a scoring system for commercial loans. Banks without a loan risk rating formula use the collective judgment and experience of the senior loan officers. They arrive at some non-quantified ranking of your loan relative to a riskless investment, such as government securities.

At the end of this chapter is a more detailed example of one approach to loan grading.

What gets a good score? Quick ratios larger than 1.0, current ratios larger than 2.5, and debt-to-worth ratios less than 0.5. All ratios better than your industry averages; consistent earnings for more than five years; after-tax profits alone equal to 1.3 or more times loan principal repayments; cash flow coverage of term debt equal to 3.0 or better; financial statements prepared by a respected accounting firm; trade suppliers reporting payments discounted to prompt; top management that is highly experienced and of unquestioned integrity.

What can you do to raise your score? Not much, if you are going to the bank tomorrow. Quite a bit as part of regularly managing your company.

Hire a respected local accounting firm. You don't have to pay for expensive audits, but pay for systems reviews and good tax advice. Have the accountants set your chart of accounts and select your fiscal accounting year to make your financials look their very best.

Ask your bank to recommend an accountant. Most likely they will give you several names. Interview them and if you don't like any of them ask the bank again for some more names. Why? Insurance. Bank credit departments have a list of accounting firms they do not trust: firms that do poor work, have questionable ethics or are uncooperative. If your financial statements are prepared by one of these unprofessional firms, you have a serious credibility problem. I hope you aren't in a real big hurry for your loan. Banks will never tell you which accountants are on this internal list. Why get sued? However, they will tell you who the good guys are.

Set up financial policies to help create a positive picture. Allow some profits to accumulate in the company. Pay your major suppliers on time and take trade discounts if you can.

Build your management and industry reputation. Collect and study information on your industry and your competitors. Participate in industry activities and trade groups. Build a reputation and referral base outside of your home town.

Be a selective but visible participant in community groups, charities, and local business associations. Network: It can't hurt to go to the local manufacturer's association monthly lunch and chat with a bank officer or a prospective customer.

The credit department at this point has finished its work. Your loan officer has reviewed the situation and decided to proceed with getting loan committee approval on your loan request. In smaller banks the loan would be presented to either the full board of directors or a loan subcommittee of the board made up of directors and bank officers.

In larger banks a senior loan committee would be made up of senior level bank officers. Only very large loans would then move from this committee to final approval from the board of directors or its appointed loan subcommittee.

As a loan officer I presented loans at all levels and as a department head served on senior loan committees. Here's how it works:

A loan presentation "package" is prepared by the loan officer and the credit department. The contents of the package can vary from bank to bank. It can be one or two pages or dozens, depending on the size and complexity of the credit. The larger packages have lengthy summaries and analyses of the company's financials, industry trend data, and cash flow projections.

The top sheet of the package is the formal loan request and summary of the loan's purpose, structure, terms, and collateral. The profit history of your deposit and loan accounts at the bank and the projected profits on the proposed loan are included.

Most banks now have profit goals or targets for each loan and each customer relationship. The setting of your loan interest rate is a function of both the degree of risk assigned by the bank and of the bank's profitability targets. Customers who always keep a bare minimum balance in their account will pay more loan interest.

The loan packages are distributed to the committee members usually in the afternoon of the day before the committee meeting. If there is a heavy agenda, the diligent committee member needs between two and four hours of reading and preparation time. I cannot recall a single committee meeting I attended where I thought every member had made adequate preparation.

The loan officer makes a verbal presentation of the request, usually taken from the loan summary sheet. Then she gives her interpretations of the financial analysis, and her personal experiences with the company and its management. The committee members will ask questions, give their reactions, and raise objections. The unprepared committee member's vote counts the same as the vote of the member who carefully read all the loan packages. The unprepared member will decide on the basis of the loan officer's presentation, the following discussion, and perhaps how some other members vote.

Loan committees are not predictable. The loan officer never knows what to expect. I have had difficult loans glide right through and apparently simple loans end up in long, drawn-out dog fights.

A vote is taken and usually majority rules. Loans can be approved, denied, or sent back because of insufficient data or analysis. Personalities of committee members come into play. Differences of lending philosophy and personal preferences for certain kinds of businesses can turn your loan into a political football. Whether the borrower is known personally or by reputation to the committee members is also important.

On difficult credits the loan officer will try to line up votes before the meeting by visiting with influential committee members. Theoretically all votes are equal, but usually the chairperson of the committee has the most clout. It is a rare loan that gets approved against the chairperson's wishes.

The secretary to the loan committee chairperson is usually responsible for rounding up sufficient committee members for a quorum. He or she is a popular person with the loan officers. It is important to know ahead of time, when taking a loan to committee, whether allies or enemies will be present.

The internal operating "atmosphere" of the committee reflects the culture of the bank. Some committees are interested in making the loan happen. They encourage and offer suggestions and alternatives to the loan officer. Other committees are like a fraternity hazing ritual. The gossip in the bank after a committee meeting is about which loan officer got chopped up, by whom, and how badly. Committees can also be merely rubber stamps for the bank's loan officers. Once a loan is turned down it rarely can be presented again to the committee. One strike and you are out. Sometimes approval is subject to some conditions, such as more collateral, a specific level of deposit balances, or different covenants in the loan agreement.

The key subjective factor in getting a loan approved is the credit reputation and presentation skills of the loan officer. Seniority always counts for a lot. Those officers who appear confident, speak well, and answer questions promptly and thoroughly do well by their customers in loan committee. I would want a loan officer who was active in Toastmasters.

Why do you want to get your loan officer out to your place of business? So she can talk positively and personally about your company. So he sees in his mind your place of business when answering questions.

Why make sure the loan officer understands your industry? So she can respond with some personal insight or anecdotal evidence that is not in the credit department package.

Why go to bank receptions, meetings, or seminars? So the loan committee members will recognize your name and have a face and a favorable association to make with it.

Why when selecting a bank do you care who is on the loan committee? Do you want a director who is a customer or a competitor of yours voting on your loan application?

The rate of interest on your loan can be arrived at in several ways. The same borrower is likely to be offered a slightly different rate by different banks in the same town. Interest rates on the same loan can vary by a larger margin from one part of the country to another, and even more widely from one type of lender to another.

Why does this happen? The balance of supply and demand for loan funds has some impact, but more on the general overall level of interest rates than on a specific loan request. Banks have elaborate procedures for determining the rate to be charged. These pricing formulae, like the risk rating systems, are not the same from bank to bank and will produce different results. Commonly the formulae include the rate paid by the bank to obtain deposits, the level of earnings needed to keep the shareholders happy, the amount of deposits the borrower will keep at the bank, and the risk rating assigned to the loan by the bank. All of these elements can differ from bank to bank in the same city or around the country. Some non-bank lenders make riskier loans on average than do banks. Their shareholders require a higher return for the higher risk.

There are two areas where you can directly impact the loan pricing formula: your risk rating and your deposit balances at the bank. The other factors are determined by forces external to the bank or by the bank's internal cost accounting and shareholder relations policies. The bank will exactly describe the impact on your loan interest rate of money left in your account at the bank. If you leave 10 percent of the loan amount on deposit with the bank your interest rate will be higher than if you left 20 percent. Your accountant will show you how to calculate if it is a good deal for you or not.

The rest of this book is about how you lower the banker's risk evaluation of your loan request.

Credit Scoring Example

This particular evaluation awards a maximum total of 36 points to each borrower from four rating categories:

Financial Statements	16 Points
Company Characteristics	8 Points
Reputation with Others	6 Points
Reputation with Bank	6 Points

Scores or point counts rank the companies:

Rank	Quality	Points
I	High	33-36
II	Very Good	28-32
III	Good	23-27
IV	Acceptable	17-22

Companies ranked less than IV are turned down for loans. The more borrowers there are wanting loans, the higher up the quality scale a company has to score to get a loan.

Each of the four rating categories is subdivided into specific components, with each component assigned a range of values.

Financial Statements: 16 Points in four components

Quality of Information: 0-4 Points

Leverage & Capital: 0-4

Liquidity: 0-4

Cash Flow/Debt: 0-4

Company Characteristics: 20 points in seven components,

then divided by 2.5 for a maximum value of 8.

Time in Business: 0-2 Points

Sales Trend: 0-4

Customer Quality: 0-2

Suppliers: 0-2

Business Cycle Impact: 0-2

Product: 0-4

Management: 0-4

Reputation with Others: 6 points in two components

Credit Agency Reports: 0-3 Points

Direct Credit Inquiries: 0-3

Reputation with Bank: 12 points in three components

then divided by 2.0 for a maximum value of 6

Time as Customer: 0-4 Points

Payment History: 0-4

Loyalty to Bank: 0-4

So we now have four rating categories that are compiled from sixteen components. Each component is further subdivided into either three or four subdefinitions for a total of 51 subdefinitions. Each subdefinition has its own point value.

So how does it work? Here are a few examples:

Under the category of "Financial Statements," the component "Quality of Information" receives from zero points if the financials are incomplete or too old, to four points if the financials are audited or prepared by a reputable accountant and all relevant or reasonable information is given.

Under "Reputation with Bank: Loyalty to Bank," zero points go to the loan applicant who scatters business over two or more banks and chases the best "deal" from one bank to another. Four points are earned if the loan applicant has all the company's loans and deposits plus the personal banking of the owners at the bank.

In "Company Characteristics: Management," four points go to a management that is considered to be experienced in the company and industry, with a good record of performance and an acceptable management succession in place. It should be pretty clear what gets zero points.

"Reputation with Others" stresses a clear payment history with at least six trade creditors and a management reputation for honesty and integrity.

It is quite possible to be turned down even with a high score. A management known to be dishonest or a debt load that the company clearly cannot carry override any score value.

In addition to the point values at least four other factors are considered in a less quantitative way: collateral, contingent liabilities, guarantees, and loan characteristics. These four other factors modify the point score in an inexact way; they can be either negative, neutral, or plus.

This credit scoring system details one bank's view of credit analysis. I think it is representative of what a borrower can expect today. The greatest emphasis is placed on reliable historical financial information and on the current financial condition of the borrowers. Sales trends, product quality, and management capacity dominate company characteristics, the second most important category.

Investigation of a borrower's reputation will extend well beyond the usual credit agency checks. Those companies that have spent some time developing a relationship with the bank and its officers have a better chance of borrowing.

Collateral is in its traditional but powerful position in the lending decision. Collateral alone is not sufficient reason to make the loan, but it is a rare loan that will be made without collateral.

Other contingent company liabilities, personal guarantees, the purpose of the loan, its repayment schedule, and administrative costs are all considered and can become deal breakers (negative) or deal makers (positive) for loans with lower scores.

Chapter 8
Seven Questions
You Must Always Answer

There are lots of businesses that want to borrow money, but from the banker's point of view there are too few qualified borrowers. There are too few good loans. Lenders have to sort through a lot of junk to find the deals that fit the needs and policies of their bank. There is a saying that you can teach someone in five minutes how to lend money, but it takes years to teach them how to get it repaid.

To get a loan you must distinguish yourself from all the losers. You must excite the loan officer. You must stand out from the crowd. You want the loan officer to know that you are different from the "typical" unprofessional and unprepared businessperson.

Seven questions are always asked in any borrowing situation.

1. How much money do you want?

2. What are you going to do with the money?

3. Why is this loan a good thing for your business?

4. Why do you need our depositors' money to do it?

5. When will you pay it back?

6. How will you pay it back?

7. What happens if your plans don't work out?

These questions apply if this is your first or your fiftieth loan. They may not be asked directly, but they are in the front of the banker's thoughts. If you cannot answer these questions to the banker's satisfaction, you will not get your loan. It is as simple as that.

Many borrowers are not ready with the answers at the time they apply for a loan. Loan officers expect this to be the case. The first visit with the loan officer is in very general terms. You usually don't get the officer's complete attention. The loan officer tries to find out in this first meeting if there is any reason to refuse the loan, and if so turns down the applicant. If there is no immediate reason to turn away the loan, then the officer is vaguely encouraging. The bank gives the borrower a checklist of information needed to analyze the loan request.

Most smaller business borrowers arrive at the bank unprepared to make a loan presentation and unable to answer the Seven Questions. If you are prepared and can answer the questions in the first two minutes of the conversation, you have immediately made a good impression. You have sent a signal to the banker that you are quite different from most small business borrowers. You have sent a signal that you can make the officer's life a little easier and the loan application less troublesome.

1. How much money do you want?

I actually have had business borrowers answer this question with another question, "How much will you lend me?" These folks rarely got to the second interview.

This question gets a lot of attention from the banker. A properly trained loan officer will frequently figure out for himself how much you need to borrow. The banker will certainly check out your proposed amount.

Answer this question with as exact a dollar amount as you can. There are some who advise asking for more than you need. Then, in case the banker trims back your loan request to a smaller amount, you will still get what you need. There are others who advise that you ask for less than you need and plan somehow on stretching it out to make do.

Both of these strategies will work against you in most cases. Obviously, if you borrow less than what you need, you have probably borrowed enough to get yourself in trouble. Then you are in the box of having to go back to the bank and ask for more. You have hurt your credibility. You look like you do not understand your business needs. Worse yet, you have made the loan officer look like he doesn't know his stuff either.

If you ask for more than you need and then, under questioning, cut back on the amount, you look like you were trying to put one over on the lender. Maybe you have some hidden expense you do not want the bank to know about, like a new bass boat or car? With either of these approaches you risk damage to your reputation as a businessperson.

Be as exact as you can and then allow an amount for errors or contingencies. The banker will understand this. The banker allows for contingencies. In fact, bankers call it an "Allowance for Bad Debts."

2. What are you going to do with the money?

Here you need to be as detailed as possible. There are only four things you can do with your new loan: buy new assets, pay off old debts and expenses, substitute debt for equity in the business, or pay for expenses needed to create new revenue.

Do not tell the banker you need the loan for working capital. An accountant will tell you that working capital is equal to current liabilities subtracted from current assets. It gets larger if you increase current assets or reduce current debt. It gets smaller if you decrease current assets or add to current debt.

In my experience, borrowers who talked about working capital meant that the company was losing money and losing cash. They wanted a loan to keep feeding this problem. They usually didn't get it.

If you are purchasing equipment, then list what kinds, from whom, what warranties are included, provide pictures or brochures. If you are building or improving physical property, include any plans and bids from the contractors you will use. If you are buying additional inventory, provide a description of your planned purchases. Bankers can be pretty good at checking on and figuring costs. They may even have some cost-saving suggestions for you.

If you are paying off old debts, list the individual creditors, the amounts owed, the collateral you pledged, why you borrowed the money in the first place, and whether any payments on the debts are behind schedule. Borrowing to consolidate debt and to get a better repayment schedule can be okay, but banks go about it very carefully. A banker hates to get suckered into bailing out another lender. This makes the new lender the "last fool" in the deal. Substituting debt for equity, for example borrowing to buy out your partner, is not considered a productive loan. These special situation loans are restricted to very strong companies.

The banker takes lending seriously and rejects borrowers who don't take spending seriously.

3. Why is this loan a good thing for your business?

You have to be able to show why your company will benefit from the loan proceeds. Banks like to make what they call productive loans: loans that result in higher volumes or better margins; loans that enable you to sell more or reduce your costs; loans that will make your company more profitable.

Debt consolidation loans may make your cash flow more comfortable, but don't add much to the bottom line. A productive loan creates new cash money to pay off the loan.

Many times with a growing company a productive loan comes after and during the growth, not before. The company has been adding to its inventory or accounts receivables as it grows, but profits aren't growing fast enough to pay for these new assets. The company needs to finance these new assets with bank debt until either the growth slows and profits catch up or until new equity capital is invested.

Do you have proof of more orders than you can fill? Do you have a large new contract in hand? Can you show the increased capacity or lower labor or operating or maintenance costs of the new equipment you are buying? Can you show the cost savings coming from your expanded office or warehouse or plant layout? Do you have a clear marketing and distribution plan for your new products? Can you show there is enough customer demand for your new products?

A loan needs to be a good idea for both the lender and the borrower. Good ideas increase profits and cash flow and repay bank loans.

4. Why do you need our depositors' money to do it?

The obvious answer is that you don't have enough money of your own and banks are where the money is. "Why don't you have enough money of your own?" is the follow-up question. This can be an easy or a tough question to answer.

Certainly some purchases, like new equipment, land, buildings and vehicles, require cash up front and a long time to pay off. Bankers know that very few companies are profitable enough or patient enough to save up and pay cash. You still must show why this is a good idea for your company. You will need some of your own cash as a down payment.

The question gets tougher if the loan is to buy or pay for already-owned inventory. Except for seasonal peaks, inventory costs should be paid by the regular profitable flow of cash or the cash cycle of the business.

Inventory is balanced or supported by your vendor credit, by your capital ownership investment, and by after-tax profits kept in the company. Most of the time an inventory loan means an out-of-balance condition in your company and you must explain that condition. Growth clearly can create an out-of-balance and out-of-cash condition. You definitely will have some explaining to do if you need money to pay for expenses such as insurance premiums or taxes. Why is your company cash not there for regular everyday operating expenses? Is it poor planning or low profits?

The question is toughest if you are asking for a straight debt consolidation and extension loan. The banker's real question is,"If you cannot pay these other debts today, why should I think you can pay my loan in the future?"

Borrowers who do not understand and cannot explain clearly why they have to borrow are common. A competent banker usually manages to pull it out of the borrower or figures it out for himself. Often the cause of borrowing is a problem, such as slow-turning inventory, a delay in customer payments on accounts receivable, too-high overhead, or bidding contracts at too-low a profit. Figure out ahead of time how to answer the question of why you need the bank's money. Put the explanation and any needed corrective steps in your loan proposal from the very start. A borrower who fails to recognize the real cause of his cash need or who is unable to convince the loan officer that she can correct it is considered too much of a risk. She will be turned down.

5. When will you pay it back?

Many years ago banks made only short-term loans—ninety days or perhaps a growing season—to finance a specific agricultural or trading transaction. It was financing a deal, not a business. You can still get a deal financed. Loans for seasonal inventories that build up and then are sold down, for contractor project financing, for interim construction loans, for import and export are all still done. When you are doing a short-term deal the timing of the repayment program is obvious. The bank and the borrower can talk ahead of time about the risk that the deal might not go through. The bank comes up with ways to reduce the amount of risk of non-payment in the deal, such as collateral, controlling documents, or requiring inspections.

Financing a business is different. A mortgage loan to buy a building, a multi-year loan to buy equipment, or a loan to pay for growing accounts receivable and inventory require the basic earning power of the business to pay them off. A projected cash flow statement is the best way to plan out a principal repayment program acceptable to both the bank and the borrower. It is the only financial statement that can begin to answer the question "When?"

The cash flow statement is more than a profit and loss statement: It traces the company's incoming and outgoing cash. It shows when excess cash from profitable operations will be there to pay off the loan. You don't have to be a math major to work out a cash flow with pencil and paper. Sample forms are available from the Small Business Administration. There are several personal computer programs that will help you put together this analysis. Most larger bank credit departments have a program they use to analyze a bigger loan request.

Even if your loan officer doesn't seem to care about this type of analysis, you should do it for yourself. It is the best way to protect yourself against the pressure of too-short a repayment program. It is the best way to avoid depending upon a loan officer willing to roll your loan over every ninety days. Some borrowers like rolling a ninety day note. They think that an agreed-upon repayment program locks them in and takes away their flexibility. This is just not correct. A repayment program protects the borrower against the bank. You are not at the mercy of a change in loan officers or a change in loan policy. You are not risking a demand for repayment every ninety days. As long as you can prepay your loan without a penalty, why not lock into a repayment program?

If you and the bank agree to a repayment program that takes several years, you still may have to sign a note for a shorter period. Banks like this "exit opportunity" where they can refuse to renew your note and ask you to pay off your loan or move it somewhere else. Even though you have been making your payments as agreed and have done nothing wrong, the bank can simply refuse to deal with you any more.

Why would this happen? Perhaps your industry is in a downturn and the bank is not confident that you can manage through it. Perhaps the bank has new owners with higher credit standards and your loan does not qualify. Perhaps loan demand is high and the bank wants to upgrade its loan portfolio by clearing out some smaller or weaker credits like you. Does this happen a lot? It happens often enough so that you need to be aware of it. Yes, you can sue. Yes, you can be difficult about it, but your business is not suing banks. And legal work can be expensive.

If you cannot get a note for the term necessary to pay the loan off, protect yourself with a simple letter of agreement. This letter reviews the terms of the loan and states that the note will be renewed at maturity, if your company has satisfactorily met the terms, conditions, and payments on the original note. You can write the letter and ask the banker to simply sign an acknowledgment. If this doesn't work, ask the bank to sign a letter agreeing to give you no less than ninety days prior notice if they do not intend to renew your loan at maturity.

Just getting the loan is often not enough. You may have to work at keeping it. From the day you get the loan, include in your plans working for its renewal. Chapter 12 has some specific suggestions on this subject.

6. How will you pay it back?

You can really hurt your loan application by being vague and unfocused in dealing with this question. Here again the banker must clearly see how she will get the depositors' money back. If it is financing for a short-term deal, be very specific about how the deal goes together. Who are the others in it? What is the anticipated timing? What are the profit margins? What are the risks that it will go bad? How will the bank get its depositors' money back?

Paying for your seasonal retail inventory buildup of snowblowers or bikinis or purchasing raw materials for a large order are acceptable deals. The loan is repaid at the end of the selling season or when your customers pay you.

Sometimes a loan can be repaid with another loan. This is most common in construction where one lender finances the construction of a project and then another lender pays off the construction loan with a long-term mortgage loan. A lot of these deals have fallen apart at the last minute. The borrower failed to meet some terms required by the long-term lender, who then backed out. This left the short-term construction lender holding the loan and holding the bag. Some banks now treat interim construction loans as an unwanted exception to their loan policies.

An occasional loan will be paid off by a new equity investment in the company at a later date. These usually short-term loans are retired with the proceeds from some type of public stock offering. This is fairly sophisticated lending and the uncertain nature of the stock market keeps most banks away from these loans.

Banks and savings and loans also make loans where the only plan to pay the loan is with the sale of the collateral itself. These are real estate, land, cattle, and oil loans. Inflation makes these loans look like sure winners, yet these asset market-value based loans can be dangerous. It was such loans that brought the collapse of a number of financial institutions. When collateral is the first or primary source of repayment and not the secondary source, then the collapse of market prices, the slowing of the economy, or the rise of interest rates may not only wipe out the value of the asset, but also drive potential purchaser/borrowers out of the market.

The point should be noted that whole industries or sectors of the economy can get "hot" and attract a lot of lenders. The mob or crowd psychology of lenders has repeated itself time and time again. Once the collapse comes, then these industries are shunned for a time by many lenders and even the best of deals have trouble getting done.

For longer-term loans, the answer of how you will repay the loan is more complicated. The bank must be sold on the lasting earning power of your business. You have to show there is excess cash flow from profitable operations. This is the only acceptable answer to this question. Excess cash is cash you don't need anywhere else in your business. The size and timing of this excess cash can be shown only with a projected cash flow statement. This projection must include each of the next twelve months and quarterly projections for the following two years.

You must convince the bank that the cash flow will be there and that it will continue for a period long enough to pay off the loan.

7. What happens if your plans don't work out?

Collateral is the traditional answer to this question. Assets are pledged to the bank when the loan is made, assets that can be sold, if necessary, to repay the loan. It is a pretty good answer. An experienced lender will tell you that collateral is rarely there when you really need it. Chapter 9 covers how to present the value of your collateral. The bank is not in the business of selling collateral. Selling collateral usually means the bank made a mistake, and no one likes to admit to mistakes.

To create a better impression and improve your chances of getting the loan, show, as part of your proposal, that you have figured out the kinds of things that could go wrong. Show that you understand how these problems could hurt your deal or your company. You know the risks of your business much better than the banker does. You don't want to leave identifying and evaluating the bad things that could happen to the banker's rich and negative imagination.

Again with a personal computer cash flow statement you can work out the damage to your company of price-cutting competition, overhead increases, delays in customer collections, or very rapid sales growth.

Estimate how likely these problems are to happen. Show what might be early warning signals that plans are being delayed or not going as planned. Explain what your options are to correct the problem or to reduce any possible damage.

Always remember that businesspeople are mostly positive; bankers are trained to be doubtful and cautious, and their training is focused to a large degree on the Seven Questions.

Chapter 9
The Test of the Five Big C's

Many industries have their own special phrases or code words. They are used to summarize or pull together significant principles of operation. The banking industry is no different.

In the preceding chapter you met the Seven Questions you must always answer. The questions are logical and objective. In this chapter you will learn about the Five C's of Credit: Character, Capacity, Conditions, Collateral, and Capital. These elements are more subjective, but equally essential to making the credit decision.

1. Character

In the lending process character means can you be trusted? It is an old-fashioned word, and perhaps to many an old-fashioned concept. It is a very practical consideration in lending.

According to press reports, a number of recent failures of banks and savings and loans is directly traceable to fraud on the part of borrowers or the owners of the financial institution. A typical loan officer does not have time to act as a warden, watching over dishonest borrowers. In conversation with the banker small mistakes can hurt you. Check your speaking habits. Try to avoid saying "to tell the truth" or "to be completely honest" or similar phrases. It plants the idea there are times when you don't tell the truth or are dishonest. Your religious convictions are not considered. Experience has taught us there are dishonest persons falsely claiming to be religious only to deceive the lender about their character. A responsible lender will turn down your loan request if your personal or business credit history, personal or business reputation, or anything else about you creates doubt that you can be trusted to pay your debts.

Personal and commercial credit checks will be ordered on you, on any partners, and on your business. The bank may want to talk to suppliers, customers, and even former employers of yours. If you are switching to a new bank, the new bank could run a credit check at your present bank. Creditors listed on your personal financial statement may be contacted. It is a serious mistake to conceal outstanding debts. Do not leave any debts off your personal or business financial statements. When this evasion is uncovered you are presumed to be a liar. It is an act of fraud and you risk losing the protection of the bankruptcy laws.

Some honest borrowers get upset by this character check. They claim that the bank acts as if the borrower cannot be trusted. They are correct. The bank does not assume you are honest and trustworthy. A bank examiner I once worked with liked to say, "Only a fool goes to bed with a snake and thinks he won't get bitten."

Your business priorities can show up in your personal financial statement. Is your business cash starved because you have personal luxury assets and lots of grown-up toys? This sends an unfavorable signal about your character. Is it any of the bank's business how you spend your money? Only if you want to borrow some of its depositors' money.

The issue is: Are you a parasite or a nutrient to your business? In tough times would you place yourself or your business first? Perhaps your business is profitable and you have been drawing out a reasonable salary, but your personal financial statement shows a small net worth and noticeable personal debts. Are you or is your spouse a spendthrift or habitual gambler? Or has your income been going for the support of aged parents or a handicapped child? The lender will want to know.

There are other elements to character as well. When a loan looks like it might be in trouble, the first question asked is, "What kind of people do we have here?" Does the borrower have the will and resolve to work through the business problems? Will the borrower continue to feel responsible for paying the bank loan? Can we safely work with this borrower or should we cut our losses right now? The moment a bank loses confidence in the borrower the party is over. The bank starts looking for a way out of the loan.

You may resent this scrutiny. You may believe that everyone should know your word and your character are sound. The lender, with too many experiences to the contrary, cannot make an exception in anyone's case.

2. Capacity

This focuses on you and on your management team, if you have one. What talents, skills, education, experience, ambition, drive, energy, commitment, and contacts do you bring to the business? What will enable your business to survive, when so many before you have quit or failed?

Part of the folklore of banking is that most small business owners are not good businesspeople. You are seen as being good at selling or manufacturing or repairing or another basic trade skill. You are not seen as being good at putting it all together and running a business. You are seen as being one- or two-dimensional and often succeeding in spite of yourself. Whether this view is true or not you will come up against it.

A straight historical personal resume is not enough. Make sure that your resume also focuses on, emphasizes, and describes your business skills, experience, and technical knowledge necessary for success in your particular business. You may have been a field superintendent for a major construction firm, but now you own a carpet cleaning franchise. What does it take to succeed in the carpet cleaning business? What did you learn in the construction industry that you can use in the carpet cleaning business?

The capable banker understands that poor business judgment is the major weakness of smaller businesses and a major cause of loan losses. Several after-the-fact studies of loans that went bad showed most were good loans at the time they were made. There were no hidden clues when the loan was made that it would not be repaid. After the loan was made business conditions changed and management lacked the ability to respond. In other cases management blundered into failure in any number of ways, such as too-rapid growth, poor credit policies, lack of insurance, etc.

Venture capitalists take much more risk than bankers. Venture firms say they prefer investing in a company with a first-class management and a second-class product, rather than investing in a company with a first-class product and a second-class management. What does your track record say about your ability to succeed? Impress the bank with the names and backgrounds of your management team before they ask for it, and include your company attorney, your accountant, and your insurance agent.

Since "excess cash flow from profitable operations" is the only way to repay most business loans, show your business management capacity by discussing how cash moves through your company. The lender is trained to think in terms of "average days' sales" in accounts receivables or "average days-purchases" in accounts payable, and "average days' sales" in inventory. Learn what these terms mean and how to use them in your business. Your accountant can help you with these terms and how to calculate them. There is more information in the Appendix.

Your answers to the questions discussed earlier, "Why do you need our depositors' money?" and "When will you pay back the loan?" will have a lot to do with how the lender judges your capacity as a businessperson.

Make sure you can identify what I like to call the "key success factors." What is it that makes a business like yours profitable? What must be done day in and day out for your business to succeed? Is it generating repeat sales, cross selling, keeping overhead down, knowing your costs accurately, after-the-sale servicing, controlling scrap? I have never met a successful business owner who could not explain the key success factors of his business. I tried never to make a loan to somebody who couldn't explain their KSFs to me.

In describing your key success factors be precise. "Better customer service" is not an acceptable answer. You must be able to describe the standards of better service and describe the means of delivering that better service. Is it overnight delivery? Answering the phone by the third ring? A generous return policy? Easy access to service engineers? An 800 number?

If you don't understand and can't describe the Key Success Factors, how can you manage them? You have failed the capacity test.

With both capacity and character, bankers take an historical perspective. The future repeats the past. If you have failed in a previous business, your capacity to succeed in a new venture is very doubtful. If you have been untrustworthy in the past, you won't be trusted today. As individuals, the bankers may believe you have turned over a new leaf, but as lenders you won't get a penny of their depositors' money.

Earlier I said it was unlikely that most bankers would really know a lot about your business. However, commonly known operating risks specific to particular industries are taught as part of credit officer training. You indicate capacity by showing an awareness of these risks and by describing how you manage your business to contain them.

3. Conditions

This is a concept closely related to capacity. Conditions are the larger factors which you as a businessperson cannot control but to which you must respond. Conditions are hard to quantify, and as a result the banker's negative imagination goes into high gear. When the lender asks a lot of "What if?" questions, she is probing the subject of conditions. You must identify and explain those local and national economic and industry conditions that influence your business.

What events and trends will help you and what can hurt you? What would be your options to respond? Conditions could include economic booms and recessions, the development of substitute products, growing foreign competition, or new manufacturing technologies. How will the new tourist theme park affect your business?

Will discounters move in on your traditional business? Will a decline in oil prices hurt your customers and cause them to buy less from you? Are there some dominant suppliers or dominant customers who can heavily impact your business?

It is of great importance that you know about your major competitors and their strong and weak points compared to you. Where do you think the bank will sell your assets if you don't make it? Who is doing well in your industry, in your town, and why? Have a strategy for handling your competition, but avoid the temptation to knock the competition in your discussions.

Many loans fail at this point in the application because the business owner is caught unprepared and has no answers to the probing questions. A banker sees risk in a business owner too tightly focused on the present and unaware of the external factors influencing their business. Borrowers must know what is going on around them and communicate this to the lender.

4. Collateral

Collateral comes immediately to the mind of a business borrower and usually in a negative way. Bankers are considered collateral hungry, wanting collateral when none is needed, demanding excessive amounts of collateral relative to the risk involved or insisting on personal assets to collateralize a business loan.

The lender's main concern is that depositors' dollars lent to your business are repaid. Collateral is the traditional risk reducer. It is a supplemental support to the loan analysis but is not the main source of repayment. Loans are repaid, most of the time, by excess cash flow from profitable operations. Collateral is the banker's favorite answer to the question, "What happens if your plans don't work out?" If you can come up with an answer to this question that does not involve the pledge of your collateral, that's great.

Do any businesses borrow unsecured? Sure, but not too many small businesses do. Unsecured borrowers usually are well-established businesses with steady earnings streams and substantial amounts of unpledged depreciating assets. These borrowers have the ability to raise additional money from sources other than banks. Such companies usually borrow for a short-term need and repay the loan in less than twelve months.

Your challenge is to maximize the value of your collateral. The better the quality and value of your collateral the more you can borrow, the fewer restrictions might be placed on your company, and perhaps the lower your interest rate. Persuade the bank that the collateral could be sold for a price reasonably close to the claimed value. If you and the bank agree that a machine is worth $100,000, how much could the bank expect to get for it at some future going out of business sale? Would there be knockdown and transportation costs, broker's or auctioneer's commissions? It is this lower or "discounted" amount that the bank wants to lend you.

The best collateral turns easily into cash and has a predictable future value. Nothing beats the bank's own certificate of deposit as collateral. Other kinds of financial assets, such as government securities and publicly traded stocks and bonds make lenders very comfortable. The worst collateral is some type of specialized business machinery that you built yourself. It is even worse if the machinery is large, heavy, anchored to the ground, and housed in a specialized single purpose building. Think of a custom-designed giant sausage-making machine inside a refrigerated warehouse.

Borrowers base their opinion of collateral value, particularly machinery, equipment, and inventory, on what they paid for the asset or what they think it would cost to replace it. The value of these assets to a going business is quite different from their value to a bank. The bank places a much lower value from the point of rapid liquidation of a failed or failing business.

Why do banks like to make car loans? Automobile collateral has its market value published monthly. There is an active market in used cars and an established dealer system to handle the sale and the paperwork. The banker looks at business collateral the same way. Is there a way to establish value? Is there a real resale market? How could the bank sell this collateral? How much could the bank expect to net from the sale? The borrower needs to help the banker with this very industry-specific information. If you can get objective support for your assets' market-ability and value, you will receive a better valuation for collateral purposes.

Assets show on your balance sheet at cost or at depreciated value. Some of your assets, usually land, may have increased in value since you bought them. You cannot change your balance sheet to show this increase, but you can bring in proof of the higher values and ask the bank to recognize the realistic value in its credit analysis.

Supply the lender with current lists of used equipment prices and comparable new equipment prices. Show proof of an active secondary market in your industry, such as name and location of used equipment dealers. Show her copies of industry publications advertising used equipment for sale. Provide a list of possible other buyers of used equipment like competitors or foreign markets. Include a copy of any equipment appraisals you have or letters from manufacturers who support an equipment resale market.

In the case of inventory, it is sometimes possible to get letters from your suppliers stating they will buy back your unused inventory at your cost, less some restocking fee. Chemicals and compounds widely used in several industries can hold a good resale value. Raw material inventory usually has a better value than work-in-process. One company I analyzed fabricated metal tool boxes from standard grades of sheet steel. Large coils of steel were delivered by truck to the plant. The moment the coils were unrolled and stamped into various flat box pieces they lost all value as collateral.

Specialized or industry-specific equipment and inventory often can be sold to or liquidated only through your competitors. So if an entire industry is having tough times, there may be no one around to pay a reasonable price for the assets of a company in liquidation. Some years you couldn't give away an oil well drilling rig of a certain size.

If you are selling to other businesses, your accounts receivable can be used as collateral. Even these are not taken at face value for collateral.

The bank will rarely use as collateral any receivables more than sixty or ninety days past due. Your current receivables are discounted downward to allow for returns and allowances. These net receivables will be discounted further to a liquidation value. Once it is known a business has been taken over by the bank, some customers stop paying and receivables lose value.

The value of your assets to you as a going business will always be more than the loan value placed upon them by a lender. What is the loan value of your assets? It all depends upon the assets themselves, your type of business, the health of your industry, and the bank involved. It is a judgment call and you should work to influence the banker's judgment.

What are some general ranges of loan value? Equipment: 30 to 60 percent; raw materials: 20 to 50 percent; work in process: 0 to 10 percent; finished inventory: 25 to 80 percent; current accounts receivable: 50 to 70 percent; land and buildings: 0 to 80 percent.

It can take almost as much time for a lender to analyze a small loan as it does to analyze a bigger loan. Collateral can be a substitute for making the thorough credit analysis of a loan applicant's industry, markets, and background. Collateral can make a small loan a "time efficient" loan. Bankers will often deny that this is done, but it is.

The business borrower must try to lower the risk-driven need for collateral and increase the perceived loan value of the available collateral to the banker.

A banker friend calls it making a professional presentation. A client of mine says you need to make the loan decision a "no-brainer" for the banker.

5. Capital

How much does the business owner have at risk? It is a measure of the owner's commitment to the business.

It is a reality that if the lender is going to lose money on a loan, then they want the borrower to hurt also. There were many individuals who bought a home with a small down payment and when times got hard mailed the key back to the lender. They walked out on the loan because they had little to lose.

A business owns assets. Assets are purchased in one of two ways: with the owners' capital or with debt, which is other people's money. The other people's money has to be repaid from excess cash flow from profitable operations. The more stable your company and the more certain its profits, the more of your cash flow can be allocated to paying off debt. This means that you can owe larger amounts of money relative to your own capital. This is called leverage. A company with lots of debt relative to its capital is said to be highly leveraged.

A public power utility with its monopoly service area and guaranteed regulated profits can carry a lot of debt. A residential heating and air-conditioning service company is a highly competitive, seasonal business, impacted by the general economic cycle. With a less certain and more variable cash flow, the service company should operate with little leverage and a good cushion of owner's capital.

The right amount of capital for your company is a judgment call. The bankers consider the reliability of your earnings, your management capacity, the growth trends of your company and comparative statistics for other companies in your industry. They form an opinion as to your personal and your financial commitment to the company.

Are you asking the bank to have more at risk in the company than you? Is there enough capital cushion to see the company through if something goes wrong? The bank may have to foreclose immediately and liquidate collateral if there is no capital cushion to protect against operating losses and a decline in asset values.

A loan decline because of insufficient equity or capital in your company is almost impossible to overcome. You must rework your presentation and perhaps change the amount of your loan request before trying again at another lender. More than likely you will require a non-bank lender such as a commercial finance company.

These five points of loan evaluation—Character, Capacity, Conditions, Collateral, and Capital—are part of basic banker conditioning. My first employer thought these five C's should be tattooed on all loan officers. Impress the points in your mind and build them into your loan request.

Chapter 10
Putting It Together

There is never a shortage of businesses that want to borrow from a bank, but many of the loan requests that a bank receives are not from suitable bank borrowers.

Even all the bankable loans do not get made. The borrower approaches the wrong bank, or the right bank, but at the wrong time. Most often the bankable loan does not get made because the borrower either creates the wrong impression or fails to support the loan request.

Let's start at the beginning. Your research has identified the right bank for you. You have done your homework and have the name of an individual loan officer. Call and make an appointment to see this officer. Even better, have another businessperson who already knows the loan officer call ahead and say she has referred you to the lender. If you are without a name and an introduction, get a copy of the bank's Statement of Condition or officer list. Identify the senior or head commercial lending officer and make your appointment with this person. In either case, with or without an introduction, your purpose is the same. To meet the officer, to give her an overview of your business, and to leave your business plan and loan proposal for review.

You need to know if your loan request fits bank policy. There is no need to waste your time if the bank has no interest in you as a borrower. Don't ask this question over the phone. It is too easy to turn someone away over the phone. Also, in person, if you have established some rapport, the banker might have some suggestions of other lenders to approach. Plan on spending fifteen to thirty minutes in this visit. If the banker wants to spend more time with you once the conversation gets going, that's great. Don't buy a new three-piece suit or a dress for the meeting, but dress suitably. This is, after all, a sales call on a particular kind of prospect. First impressions do count.

You should convey a positive attitude that says you are worthy of credit, professional in your approach to borrowing, and interested in building a relationship with the bank. Avoid putting the banker under heavy pressure to decide. Communicate your expectation that the decision making process will move forward in a prompt, businesslike way.

Make it clear that you do not expect an answer until after the proposal has been analyzed and the banker has been out to see your place of business. Explain the bare bones of the deal: purpose, amount, repayment period, and available collateral. Be prepared to answer briefly but clearly the Seven Questions.

This information up front gives the lender a frame of reference. Does your request fit current loan policy? Are you in the wrong loan department? Is another officer more skilled in your industry? Should someone else join the discussion? Putting the deal on the table, up front, focuses the discussion.

Seek agreement on a time, within the next few days, when you can call to set an appointment for the loan officer to tour your business. Ask if the banker would like to have your accountant or any others present at that visit to answer questions and clarify any points covered in the loan proposal. This approach begins to set the timetable for the bank and shows that you have taken a professional approach to preparing the loan proposal.

It might be a time-saver to cover several banks in town at the same time with your loan proposal; however, when a credit check is ordered on your business, the report shows that the other banks are checking your credit as well. This could start some competition for your business, but most of the time this is not a good idea.

Banks don't like being played off against each other. I have seen a loan turned down for no other reason than it was being heavily "shopped" to a number of banks at the same time. It is better, but more time consuming, to work with one bank at a time. If there is something wrong with your proposal that you can fix, what you learn from the first turndown might get you a positive response at the next bank.

The physical appearance of your loan proposal is important. With personal computers and word processing programs there is no reason for a sloppy proposal with errors and misspelled words. Poor quality copies suggest that you are shopping the proposal around to a lot of banks. Don't go overboard with leather covers and such either. Give the banker at least two complete sets of your entire proposal, one for the credit department to analyze and one for the officer's personal use. Papers get lost in banks. An extra copy can speed things along. With his own copy the banker can work on your loan without having to remove your proposal from the credit department files.

In putting together your loan proposal, it is safe to assume that the banker knows very little about your industry and of course, nothing at all about your company. Even if the banker has some knowledge, others in the bank who will be participating in the analysis and decision do not. The more your presentation can explain your industry and personalize your business, the better. Be sure to include, perhaps in a separate folder, sales material, pictures of products that are in use or are being manufactured, newspaper articles or other publicity, annual reports, and recent news releases. If your industry has a trade magazine or a newspaper include several copies. Annual reviews or forecast of the industry and new developments and articles that support your reasons for borrowing are especially valuable.

Accounting firms, the Small Business Administration, and many financial authors have suggested outlines for a loan proposal. All are useful and quite similar, but the information communicated and the impression created are more important than the format. A written loan proposal, regardless of its format, is aimed at the Seven Questions and the Five C's of Credit. I prefer the following organization:

1. **The Deal**
   In a nutshell

2. **Management**
   Character and capacity

3. **Business Description**
   Condition
   Why is this a good thing to do?

4. **Financials**
   Capital
   Why do you need our depositors' money?

5. **Purpose and Amount**
   How much do you want?

6. Financial Projections and Repayment
Collateral
How will you pay it back?
When will you pay it back?
What happens if something goes wrong?

7. Summary
At a maximum a one page restatement of the major supporting points from each of the preceding sections.

Section 1: The Deal

The first section of your proposal should be a summary of the deal. This is the purpose of your meeting and the purpose of the proposal. There is no need to be coy about it. The lender wants to know this information. It is his job. Put it up front.

In as brief a statement as possible, describe the amount needed, what you intend to do with it, why this will be good for your company, how you will pay it back, when you will pay it back, and the collateral available.

Then give a quick snapshot of your company: annual sales, profits, number of employees, and who owns the company. Describe your business in simple terms and language. Use no industry or product jargon in an attempt to impress; instead, capture the personality of your company in a few sentences.

Section 2: Management

Capacity: Do you have what it takes to run your business profitably? Character: Can you be trusted? These are major concerns to the lender and are "soft," non-numbers issues. Start building your case early.

In the proposal, describe the management organization structure of the company. The business is an extension of the strengths, weaknesses, and personality of the owner, even in larger corporations. Describe who owns the company. Identify the key personnel, their function and major areas of contribution to profitable operations. Who is capable of running the business if you are not there? Also, cover any key officer insurance programs and any buy-out agreements among the management team or shareholders.

Set up a separate "Personnel Appendix." Prepare a solid resume for yourself and other key personnel. Emphasize in these resumes not static job history, but the skills learned, capabilities acquired, and experience gathered. Emphasize in the text how these are important to the successful operation of the current business. Include a table of key personnels' salaries, benefits, and company ownership position. Include information about any industry awards or other recognition received and any positions of business, community, or church leadership you have held. If you are about to hire additional management, describe the kinds of skills you are seeking. Include the names, addresses, and phone numbers of your accountant, attorney, insurance agent, and any consultants.

The bank's evaluation of you and your management team is an important element of the risk analysis. Can you cause the company to repay the loan? Can you get the customers, make the profitable sales, collect your receivables, manage your employees, and on and on and on?

Your personal financial statement needs to be part of the package. It can be included in a separate folder outside of the proposal to maintain confidentiality within your company. Most banks follow a similar format. Get a bank form ahead of time, but retype it to personalize it. Your statement should be dated within thirty days of the proposal. Support the value of significant personal assets with either cost at date of purchase or a current appraisal. All personal debt should show current balance, lender, original date, interest rate, payment schedule, and collateral pledged to the loan. List any debts not in your name which you have guaranteed or to which you have pledged collateral. Also include detail on personal insurance policies, such as carrier, amount, beneficiary, owner, and cash value.

Sign and date your personal financial statement. Falsifying information is a serious offense. Some forms state that if the personal financial statement proves to be inaccurate or incomplete in any respect, the bank may declare all your loans and any loans that you have guaranteed immediately due and payable.

You will also need to include copies of your personal income tax returns for at least the past three years. The bank will compare your reported income to your company salary and benefit schedule. Banks have very little interest in dealing with a borrower in tax trouble. The Internal Revenue Service is powerful, can seize assets, and disrupt the running of the business. All of this personal information is required of anyone else signing personally or guaranteeing the note.

The bank will order a personal credit report on you and on other signers or guarantors. Beat them to it. Review the reports before you complete your loan proposal. Correct any inaccuracies or file your permitted response to disputed or negative information at the credit bureau.

The bank will also order credit reports on your business. Again beat them to it. Clean up the reports with the reporting agency ahead of time where you can. If problems remain on your business credit report, prepare a brief explanation in the appropriate section of the loan proposal, usually when discussing suppliers and trade credit. Include the name, phone number, and address of quality character and capacity references with your resumes. These would be people and organizations who can relate positively to you and your company, for example former employers, successful former employees, former bankers, industry experts, trade association leaders, or educators.

Section 3: Business Description

Here the proposal should deal with business and industry conditions. It should also clearly make the case for the proposed loan. The loan proceeds are to be used in a particular way. Why is this a good idea? What are the short-term and long-term benefits to the borrower? Why does this loan make sense at this time for your company?

Do not underestimate the importance of this section. There is no right length, but it is likely to be the largest narrative section of the proposal. The loan is to be repaid by the successful operation of the business. Besides the loan request at hand, the bank is hoping to build a long-term profitable relationship as well.

An understanding of business and industry operations must support the reality and credibility of the financial mechanics and associated risks detailed in the fourth section, Financials, and the sixth section, Financial Projections and Repayment. Understanding the business also influences the perceived risk that assets pledged as collateral will lose their value or that business costs will become unmanageable.

Frequently borrowers assume that the banker either knows all about their business and industry or doesn't care to learn. Yet this is the area where the borrowers have the most knowledge and the banker the least knowledge. Provide as much information and detail as you think is necessary. Don't pad or repeat yourself. If your business is the only one or the first of its kind in your community, the banker has no point of reference. You have a problem. Imagine trying to find bank financing in central Texas for an ostrich breeding operation.

In such a case, make the effort through your suppliers or trade association to locate and meet other people in your business. Learn where they bank and where they borrow. Get permission to refer the banks you plan to approach to these lenders.

Bankers usually trust other bankers more than they trust potential borrowers. It is critical that communications take place so they can learn about your industry and your opportunities for success.

Describe your product or service

- How long have you been in business?
- How do you make your product?
- What is your niche in the market?
- What benefits do you sell?
- What warranties or guarantees do you offer?
- How do you price your product or services?
- Do you have any unique features or benefits? Patents? Copyrights? Trade secrets?
- Which of your products produces the most sales? The most profits?
- What have been the most significant changes in your industry and in your business in the past three years?
- What changes will take place in your industry in the next several years?
- How will your company have to change in the next several years?
- What is the real key to making money in your business?
- What distinguishes the high profit companies from the low-profit companies in your industry?

Describe your customers:

- Who is a typical customer?
- How do you acquire customers and how many do you have?

- Who are your largest customers?
- Who are your most profitable customers?
- Why do your customers buy from you instead of your competitors?
- What are your marketing, advertising, and sales strategies?
- What are your selling terms? Are you giving discounts?
- How do you distribute your product to your customers?

Describe your competitors:

- Who are your major competitors?
- What is happening to your market share? Why?
- How are you different from your competitors?

Describe your suppliers:

- Who are your key suppliers?
- Who are your backup suppliers on essential items?
- What are your suppliers' terms? Are you taking discounts?
- Have you ever experienced supply shortages? Why?

Describe your labor force:

- How many employees do you have?
- What is your employee turnover rate?
- What are the major skills required of your workforce?
- How does your pay scale compare to other local companies? To your competitors?
- Where and how do you find new employees?
- What are your labor relations like? Are you unionized? Subject to work stoppages or strikes?

Describe your equipment and physical facilities:

- Where are you located?
- Do you own or lease your facilities?
- When does your lease expire? What are the renewal terms?
- Do you have enough room for storage? Future expansion? What insurance coverage do you carry?
- What are the major items of equipment used?
- Do you have excess production capacity?
- How big is your order backlog?

Set up an "Equipment Appendix." Include a brief description of all owned and all leased equipment. Include serial numbers, dates of purchase, purchase prices, current estimates of value, financing or leasing terms. Include a copy of all equipment and premises leases.

Miscellaneous:

- If your office and accounting procedures are automated, identify the equipment and software used.

- Provide a schedule and brief description of key internal management, production, and sales reports.

- Explain any current lawsuits.

- What else do you think is important for the lender to understand about your company? About your industry? About you?

The last paragraphs should say essentially the same things as the first: the purpose of the loan and the benefits to the company of the borrowings. A loan needs to be a good idea for both the lender and the borrower. Good ideas increase profits and cash flow and repay bank loans.

Section 4: Financials

This section is to a large degree historical (What do your numbers look like?) and interpretative (How did they get that way?).

The lender wants to know how much of your money and that of any other stockholders is at risk in the company. He wants to know how rapidly your company earned profits in the past and what was done with those profits. How much capital is committed to the company? How much of a capital cushion is there to provide safety against future losses? How is the risk of loss shared between the owners and the lenders?

Borrowers are usually quite clear about how they intend to spend the loan: equipment, inventory, for example. They understand why it is a good idea. A banker wants to know why the money described in the deal or loan request cannot be found within the company or won't be supplied by the current stockholders. Why do you need the depositors' money?

If the borrowing need is caused by some problem such as declining profitability, slow collection of receivables or by past policies, heavy owner's withdrawal of profits, or high overhead, then the loan proposal must also outline the steps, the timetable, and the targeted results needed to correct the problem.

This section should contain at least the past three years' income statements, balance sheets, and cash flows. If your business has a definite seasonal sales pattern, include the same data for seasonal highs and lows.

If it has been more than sixty days since your financial year-end, provide interim financial statements. I lost a lot of confidence in a potential borrower who showed up in my office in mid-June with December 31 financials. How could he know what was going on in his business? Ideally, you should be getting a monthly income statement and a balance sheet within thirty days of month-end.

Hand a commercial loan officer a set of financial statements and watch her eyes. She'll start with the income statement and go right to the bottom line. Are you profitable?

Then she will read upward several lines to interest expense. Last she'll make a quick search for depreciation expense and any other non-cash expenses. Then the lender moves on to the balance sheet. First to the lower righthand corner. How much long-term debt? How much owners' equity? Next to the upper left corner. How much cash? Accounts receivable? Inventory? Then to the right. How much in accounts payable? In current maturities of long-term debt?

Why in this order? Because you are there to borrow. The commercial loan officer's training is to first check out the level of debt your company is carrying now, and the flow of cash to service trade credit and loans.

Finally, the officer will look for a Statement of Cash Flow to confirm her preliminary evaluation of your company's debt service capacity. I say "finally," because for many years we didn't expect to find such a statement. When we did, it was most often inadequate for loan analysis. If your basic financial statements are not prepared according to Generally Accepted Accounting Principals (GAAP), the banker considers them to be less reliable and will penalize your loan with a higher interest rate.

If the officer is thinking collateral, the next several questions will be about your inventory, accounts receivable, and equipment.

The loan officer's training also says: The past is a predictor of the future. All major operational decisions show up in the financial statements. Therefore, the lender will have a lot of questions about your past, current, and projected financial statements and how you operate your company. Your goal is to answer most of those questions before they are asked.

You must thoroughly understand the financial statements yourself. If the data is not comparable from one period to another because you changed accounting periods, or methods of inventory valuation, or made major product line changes, explain it in your proposal. It is worth paying your accountant to restate and reconcile these kinds of differences.

Banks do not like loose ends. Poorly presented and inconsistent historical financials create the suspicion that the business lacks financial controls and that management is unconcerned about the numbers.

Many firms have an outside accountant come in once a year to review the internal bookkeeping and prepare income taxes. I always wanted to see the list of correcting or adjusting entries made by the accountant at that time. I also wanted to see any suggestions for improvement the accountant made. These gave me some clues about the accuracy of the company-prepared interim financial reports.

If you don't provide financial statement continuity and comparability, the bank's credit department will try to work it out on its own. This can extend the time required for analysis and delay the decision making process. A small loan request without outstanding quality collateral that requires a lot of restatement and analysis work can get turned down. It is simply not worth the effort involved.

Comparability also includes measuring your company against the other companies in your industry. In Chapter 6 I discussed the Robert Morris *Annual Statement Studies* and how a bank uses them to look at your company.

Ratios are not mysterious or difficult to understand. They are either unfamiliar or not used very much by business owners as a management tool. This is not too surprising. The only people really interested in numbers and in business for themselves are accountants. It is the rare borrower who understands the impact of ratios in the analysis of a loan request.

The Financial Section must include a discussion of your most important ratios from the Balance Sheet and Income Statement. Explain why any trends or significant changes in your ratios have occurred. If your business ratios are quite different from those of your industry, explain why. Point out your strong points and show how you are working on your weaker points.

Your loan proposal should include supporting information: a schedule of all debt, including lender, original date, interest rate, terms, and collateral pledged. Include a copy of notes, security agreements, and loan agreements. Being one of several lenders is uncomfortable. The banker wants to know all the other players and what cards they hold. Notes and security agreements should be indexed to your equipment list appendix as described in Section 3 and an aged listing or due date analysis of your accounts receivable. Lenders believe companies that do not follow the due date and past due status of customer receivables are financially backward. If your receivables listing is not automated and available upon demand, you lose points.

If your receivables are concentrated (50 percent or more) in ten or fewer customers, and receivables are part of the collateral picture, provide some background details on these customers. Who are they? Where are they located? What is their line of business? What is their credit rating? What are their pay habits with you? Do the same on any other customer who accounts for more than 5 percent of your receivables.

Provide information on your credit approval, invoicing, and collection policies and procedures. Include a copy of the credit application you complete on each of your credit customers.

Include an aged listing of your accounts payable. The lender will compare this to the credit report ordered on your business. The bank wants to know if the loan is really intended to bail out some of your other lenders or trade creditors. It wants to know if your business is sufficiently profitable to handle credit responsibly. The bank has a subtler reason for wanting borrowers to stay up to date with trade creditors. If the bank decides the loan is weakening, it can ask for additional payments or advance less against revolving collateral. The borrower can get the cash by slowing payments to other creditors or "riding the trade." The bank wants to always be Paul so you can borrow from Peter.

The financials should make clear how the inventory was valued and provide a separate schedule for raw materials, work in process, and finished goods. The prepared borrower is the one who can list approximately 20 percent of the items that account for about 80 percent of the inventory value. The inventory schedule shows item description, item count, and value for any class of items that makes up more than 10 percent of inventory value. If inventory is a significant portion of your operation, the banker will be interested in details on purchasing, insurance, inventory control, invoicing, and the frequency of physical inventory.

Section 5: Purpose and Amount

In this section you must clearly pinpoint how much money you need and how and when you will spend it. This section ties exactly to the earlier description in Section 1, "The Deal."

You should repeat and expand upon one or more of the four uses of borrowed money: to buy assets, to replace other loans or credit, to replace an equity investment, or to pay for expenses needed to create new revenue.

Banks like to make productive loans. Loans that result in increased sales, stronger cash flow, and higher profits.

State the exact amount you wish to borrow. If there is some uncertainty, state the amount and then include an extra amount for contingencies. Explain how you figured the loan amount and support it with plans and bids from contractors, price quotes from suppliers, and price lists from vendors.

Justify how you determined the contingency amount. Picking a percentage of the loan amount out of the air is a fairly common but not very useful method. The impressive borrower justifies a number based upon knowledge of his business and the industry. Past swings in raw material prices or the company's own track record in sales forecasting or probable delays caused by vendors are some of the reasons that provide realistic dimensions to the contingency amount.

Clearly identify any debts that will be paid off with the loan. Lending money to bail out another creditor always concerns a banker. The lender will spend a great deal of time analyzing this portion of the deal. Sometimes the banker will suggest enlarging the loan request to take out other borrowers. Paying off another lender can give the new lender a more secure loan, with first position on additional collateral. Other times it is more efficient for the banker to make a larger loan.

It may not be to your advantage as a borrower to increase the requested loan amount to pay off another lender. The old loan might be at a lower interest rate or on a more favorable payment schedule than the proposed new loan. You might have substantial equity or borrowing power in the assets pledged to the old loan that you want to hold in reserve for a later time. Maybe you are thinking about selling the assets pledged to the old loan. Rolling existing debt into a new loan is negotiable, but if the banker brings up the idea he usually feels strongly about wanting to make it a condition of the loan.

Back up your loan request to increase your current assets, inventory, or accounts receivable with well-reasoned sales forecasts in the following section.

Section 6: Financial Projections and Repayment

There are only four ways to repay a loan: with another loan, by liquidating or selling off assets, by additional equity investment in the company, or with excess cash flow from profitable operations. Seasonal business loans are repaid by the successful sale or liquidation of the inventory asset or by the collection of the accounts receivable asset. A defaulted loan, one not paid as agreed, can be repaid by the repossession and liquidation of assets assigned as collateral to the loan.

The planned repayment of a loan with another new loan or with new equity invested in the company is relatively rare. The typical business loan is repaid with excess cash flow from the profitable operations of the company.

Excess cash flow is cash, not accounting profits. Cash not needed in the business to pay bills, replace assets, pay to owners and shareholders, or finance additional growth. The amount of this excess cash flow when it is created by the business, its certainty and reliability, determine the loan repayment schedule and influence the amount of collateral required.

Collateral pledged to the loan is a secondary source of repayment. It is there in case something goes wrong and the cash flow from business operations cannot repay the loan. With the exception of cash deposits, assets pledged as collateral change in stated value over the life of the loan. Some of these changes are artificial such as equipment depreciation. Others are a function of business operations, such as total inventory and accounts receivable. Not all changes in collateral value show up in the company's financials. Land is always shown at cost, not market value.

Financial projections in the loan proposal must take all of this into account and also clearly show the amount and purpose of the loan request. This requires the preparation of projected profit and loss statements, projected balance sheets, and cash flow projections for the same future periods. All projected statements should be on a monthly basis, at least for the first year, but preferably for the first two years, and quarterly thereafter for at least three more years, if the loan will run that long.

Time and time again I meet with disappointed loan applicants. They have been to several banks with a specific loan request to finance the expansion of their business. When I ask to see their projections, all they have to show is a twelve month profit and loss projection. Often, this even fails to include interest expense on the requested loan. They are only telling the bank how much money they want. This is not enough.

Without a balance sheet projection, it impossible to see exactly what has been purchased with the loan or the impact of sales growth on business assets and liabilities. Without a balance sheet projection, it is impossible to trace the relative value of the business assets to the loan principal owed. Remember, the lender is also applying a judgment discount factor to the stated value of your assets to arrive at the collateral loan value. The loan value of assets changes as raw materials are converted by the manufacturing/sales cycle into accounts receivable. The lender wants to forecast this ahead of time. Without a cash flow, it is impossible to show how and when the loan will be repaid.

The financial projection and repayment section of your loan proposal will be a principal focus of the bank's credit analysis. Do a bang-up job on this section. You want to get the bank officer's attention, to accelerate the processing of your loan application, to differentiate yourself from the other loan applicants, and to improve your chances dramatically of getting your loan approved. There is no better way. This section appears to be primarily numbers, but the assumptions behind the numbers and the relationship between the numbers and the previous sections are the truly critical elements. Make solid supportable assumptions based upon past performance and any planned changes. Extend these assumptions into well-reasoned projections.

Then spend your time considering alternative assumptions and projections to define the limits of risk. What can go wrong, and how badly can it go wrong? What impact does this have on the company and your ability to repay the loan? Determine the "best," the "worst," and the "most likely" to happen.

The numbers crunching resulting from this process can easily be done on any one of a number of personal computer software packages. Your accountant should have such a program and be able to help with the projections. Do not design one of these programs from scratch. Your time is better spent running your business. Why run the risk of misleading errors that can destroy the credibility of your projections?

Several years ago a friend asked me to review a financing proposal he designed on his personal computer. He intended to use the proposal to interest a venture capital firm in financing a leveraged buyout. I saw an obvious arithmetic error that substantially changed the amount of financing required. "Thank God," he said. "I haven't shown it to anyone important yet."

The biggest advantage of these software programs is the ability to change assumptions or financial policies. You see immediately the impact these changes have on your projected financials. You can, just by messing around with the computer model, identify the few items, the "critical variables," that have the greatest impact on your profitability, on your cash flow, and on your ability to repay the loan. Expensive consultants call this a sensitivity analysis.

Most banks have these computer programs and will run your numbers through them as part of the credit analysis. Why? To see if you made any calculating errors in your presentation. More importantly, to figure out for themselves the critical variables and your cash flow debt service break-even point. They want to know how much your sales can drop off or your expenses can increase before you are no longer able to create enough cash to repay the loan. The bankers even have their own acronym for this: CRD, Critical Revenue Decline. When it happens the loan turns to crud (CRD). If they are going to know this, shouldn't you? And if you know you are going to be asked about it, shouldn't you have your answers ready?

Even better, include in the projections your estimates of this downside risk and your analysis of the likelihood it could happen. For example, "Sales would have to drop below the lowest level in the past three years before debt repayment would be endangered. Reductions in service staff levels and direct labor expenses would support debt repayment ability at even lower sales levels."

The projections are prepared assuming the loan has been made. For example, if it is an equipment loan, show the additional equipment on the balance sheet, increase your depreciation charges accordingly, show interest expense in the income statement, and loan principal repayments in the cash flow. Use a realistic interest rate. Make some anonymous phone calls to local banks. Ask what general range of interest rates they charge for a loan of the size, type, and term you will be needing. Banks do not like to answer this kind of question over the phone, but persist. Use a rate near the high end of the range in your calculations. Explain and show the impact of the new equipment on output, on increased sales, on reduced expenses, and improved profits. The ability to sell this increased output was supported in Section 3, "Business Description."

Go through the projected financials and write a sentence or two for each line item except the most obvious ones. This sentence is to explain and provide support for every assumption built into the financials. For example, accounts receivable will continue to turn over at the current thirty-seven day average. Gross margin will improve 0.5 percent from new machine labor scheduling efficiencies and 0.3 percent by qualifying for additional discounts under new vendor volume purchase programs. Strongly support and explain projected increases in sales, both in this section and in the "Business Description" section. Too often projected sales increases look like numbers just grabbed from anywhere.

Explain why you can expand your market, how you know there are additional customers and sales to be gained, how many new customers or additional sales to existing customers it will take to meet your estimates. What will you do to make these new sales happen? How will you track your progress toward these targets?

Are you doing the lender's or credit analyst's work for him? I certainly hope so! The fewer questions and blanks you leave for the banker's negative imagination to fill in, the better off you will be. Think of it this way: You lose points if you are asked a question and do not know the answer. You lose fewer points if you are asked a question and know the answer. You *make* points if the thoroughness of your presentation makes the question unnecessary.

Industry comparative ratios are used with your historical financials and also with your projected financials. If your projected ratios show a substantial shift in value from recent levels or a change in trend, the bank will pick up on it. Again, beat them to it and explain the changes in your proposal.

You have spent some time with your computer model, either directly or with the help of your accountant. You are fairly confident that you have reasonably identified three future scenarios for the period covered in your forecast time frame: a Best case, the Most Likely, and the Worst case.

You have thought about and have some feeling for the odds that any one of the three cases will actually happen. Maybe one in ten for "best" case, six in ten for "most likely," and three in ten for "worst-case." Events with less than a one in ten probability should be of concern only to insurance companies.

A good loan officer and credit analyst will also work these probabilities out on his own. Your odds will almost always be more optimistic than his. Do not compare odds with him, unless he asks. I usually asked and then adjusted the borrower's response toward the negative.

You have printed out and studied the three sets of financial statements—balance sheet, income statement, cash flow—for each of the three alternatives. Now how much do you show the lender?

If none of the three, or only the "best" case, generates enough cash to repay the loan in three to five years, don't even bother with the bank unless you have lots of good quality collateral. Otherwise, always include "most likely" here in Section 6 and make references to "best" and "worst" in the narrative where needed. The banker will not spend a lot of time reviewing the "best" case. His main concern about the "best" case is whether or not it will require the bank to lend more money and will it change the repayment schedule or the loan to collateral coverage shown in the "most likely" case. Cover these points in this section's narrative. Usually it can't hurt to include the "best" case statements as a separate appendix. Especially if the balance sheet shows lots of cash on deposit at the bank.

The weaker your repayment ability under "most likely," the more important the "worst" case becomes to the lender and to you.

If the "worst" case can handle the loan easily, state that in the narrative and put the projected statements in a separate appendix. Understand that the banker will still review them with some attention, trying to disprove that the "worst" is really that good. If the "worst" case cannot handle the loan, it will become a near 100 percent certainty in the banker's mind. Still, put it in the appendix. Don't be surprised if you spend more of your discussion time with the lender on the details of the one in ten chance "worst," than on the eight in ten chance "most likely." You had better be able to make a good case for a very low probability of the "worst" occurrence and for the soundness of the bank's collateral position. The banker will want to know, if you can identify some early warning signs that you might be heading toward the "worst." Do you have a plan to change your strategies, cut costs, or provide more collateral?

Section 7: Summary

The summary should pull together, in less than one page, the most important points from each of the preceding sections. A well-prepared summary will be copied by the credit department right into the written loan analysis for presentation to the loan committee.

Common mistakes to avoid in your loan proposal include:

- Failure to communicate clearly your understanding of the key success factors in your business.

- Failure to think through projections in specific detail. For example, how many customers per day with an average sale of what dollar amount do you need to meet your projections?

- Inadequate analysis of your competitors and how your business creates a competitive edge.

- No description of internal financial and management controls, checks, and balances.

- No identified milestones or targets to serve as check points on your projections and progress.

- Inadequate and unsupported current or projected financial statements.

It is your responsibility to come up with all the information, appendices, statements, and projections described in this chapter. You lose points and look amateurish every time you come up short, every time you cannot answer a question or have to go back for something else, every time you have to explain why numbers don't hang together or explain discrepancies and discontinuities. Worse than that, you look like potential trouble.

In some meetings with the banker to discuss your financials and projections you should have your bookkeeper, accountant, or financial consultant along. It is of critical importance that you do most of the talking, not your accountant or outside consultant. If you did the projections correctly and had the major part in putting them together, you should be able to answer at least 80 percent of the banker's questions. Make sure you are thoroughly briefed before going into these meetings.

Does this all sound like a real pain in the assets? You bet it does! Can you avoid it? Perhaps, but not likely, especially if you are borrowing amounts that are significant for the size of your business.

Answer your banker's questions honestly, openly, with as much patience as you can muster. Sharing information with the lenders builds confidence and builds a sense of partnership and commitment. And if they want to see your business, give them a great tour. Show how you process orders, make your products, find new customers, watch the competition, and collect your accounts. The bankers want to meet your key personnel, see if your equipment looks well maintained, understand your work flow, and see if you have an orderly and efficient company.

I understand that these efforts appear to be distractions from the basic business, yet a businessperson will spend days on some small improvement in the company's product or months working to win a new account. It is all just a matter of priorities. Your goal is to convert that loan officer into an informed, enthusiastic advocate for your loan. You may find it hard to believe, but the banks do want to make loans. They do want to help people succeed. It is a great feeling to be able to say "Yes."

The well-prepared loan applicant will be the successful borrower. Some of my clients have said, "I don't want to go through all this. Just have them give me the money and leave me alone." Banks don't work that way anymore and probably never will again.

Chapter 11
It's Only Negotiable
Before You Sign

Congratulations! Your loan has been approved. The banker says there are just a few details to iron out, some papers to sign, and you will have the money.

In their eagerness to get the money and get on with running their business, which is much more interesting than dealing with the bank, borrowers seriously underestimate the importance of these concluding steps. Both the borrower and the lender have spent time on the proposal. They have gotten to know each other and now have some emotional investment in the deal. Bankers, however, have looking over their shoulders an interesting cast of characters: lawyers with court-tested "boilerplate" borrowing forms and agreements; loan review officers with grading forms to complete; collateral clerks with checklists to ensure clear rights to all pledged collateral; and credit analysts comparing the actual loan closing terms with those approved by the loan committee.

The borrowers on the other hand have no such set of restraints. In fact, they may even have made business commitments assuming the money will be coming as promised. They are ready to move on. But now matters casually mentioned earlier, tentative terms and possible conditions of the loan suddenly reappear with a greater degree of importance and urgency. Remember, unlike personal or consumer credit there is no Truth-In-Lending Act to protect the business borrower. Business owners have the obligation to look out for themselves.

When you show up at the bank for your loan closing, never sign a bunch of papers you have never seen before and leave with only a check or deposit ticket for the loan proceeds in your hands. The bank would not mind, but you might regret it later on. Always ask for draft copies ahead of time. Read them carefully at your office without a room full of people watching you. Review the drafts with your lawyer. Always take copies with you of everything that you have signed. Do not allow the bank to mail you your copies later on. Sometimes they don't mail them. If problems or disagreements arise later, you do not want the bank controlling the disputed documents. Simple mistakes happen all the time: wrong dates, wrong amounts, misspelled names, and wrong company officer titles. All these should be cleared up beforehand.

Even if you did not read the documents or did not understand them, you are bound by them. It takes the agreement of both parties to change the deal once the papers are signed. Sometimes this doesn't happen. Even more importantly, be sure you understand the terms and conditions that bind you and your company. Loan officers move around and bank loan policies change. Regardless of verbal promises and statements, the bank is bound to do no more than what is stated in the signed documents.

The documents should require the bank to give you reasonable notice if they are going to move against you in any way or seek to change the original terms of the loan. If they can demand payment in full simply because the loan is "deemed insecure," it doesn't matter that the bank has never done it before. Do you want to be the first example?

Cross-default and cross-collateralization clauses are important to the borrower who has more than one loan at the same bank. In effect, these clauses in the note and in the collateral agreements tie all your loans into one big loan with one big collateral package. If you fall behind or default on one loan, then all your loans on the bank's books are in default. All loans can be declared immediately payable.

The collateral on one loan is automatically cross-pledged to all your present and future loans. If you have a loan on a delivery truck, you can't keep it current and let the loan on the unneeded forklift go unpaid. The bank can take both the truck and the forklift and sell them to pay both the forklift and the truck loans.

You may have more than one company or trade style that makes these cross agreements inappropriate. Unacceptable intercompany contingent liabilities might be created. This is why you have a business lawyer. These types of clauses are negotiable only before all the papers are signed. They give the bank a very strong hand. If you can avoid being cross-tied, do it.

In most cases, if your business is a corporation or partnership you are expected personally to guarantee the loan. Some borrowers really object to this, but it is usually very difficult to avoid. However, everything is negotiable before the papers are signed. At all costs, make sure you clearly understand just exactly what your guarantee covers. The bank's view is that a business owner should be willing to guarantee 100 percent of all business debt. It will ask for a blanket guarantee. Banks feel this keeps the owner focused on the business and will discourage him from walking away, leaving the bank holding the bag on a bad loan. Additionally, your spouse may be asked to personally guarantee the loan, to prevent shifting family assets out of the reach of the bank.

There are two separate issues at play. One is personal, your character, and the other is financial, your business credit worthiness and the collateral supporting the loan. If your business has a track record of operating profitably and paying its bills on time, there is less need for a personal guarantee. If the loan is strong and well collateralized, there is little financial need for your guarantee as a third source of repayment. Then it is a matter of persuading the bank as to your strength of character and resolve to succeed with the business.

If the loan collateral from the business is not enough to satisfy the bank, then your personal assets as additional collateral are needed to make the loan work. The bank really does not separate the assets of the business and the personal assets of the business owner in its thinking. It views these two sources of collateral pretty much as just two different pockets in the same pair of pants. Your personal guarantee of the whole loan puts virtually all your personal assets into the deal. To avoid this, ask to pledge only specific personal assets to make up the collateral shortage. Or try to negotiate a personal guarantee that is less than the total loan, in effect equal to the collateral shortfall.

Can you negotiate a guarantee that over time reduces as a percent of the loan? After all, if you are making your payments on time, is not the risk reduced by the improved collateral coverage and loan payment performance?

Also at issue is when the bank can call upon you as guarantor for payment. When can the bank ask you to liquidate personal assets to pay down your company loan? Can they call in your guarantee if they only "feel insecure" about your company's ability to pay the loan? Or only after the note is ninety days past due? Or only after it has closed your business down, sold all the business collateral, and is still owed money?

What if there is more than one guarantor? Do each of you guarantee all of the loan? A fixed dollar amount? Or a percentage of the outstanding balance? Just because you and your co-owner are both guaranteeing the same loan doesn't mean the bank won't ask each of you individually to guarantee all the loan.

Outside third parties, relatives, friends, or business associates, can also guarantee your business loan. They will be scrutinized closely as well. Check with your lawyer to make sure, but most of the time you can pay these guarantors a fee for "lending" you their credit strength. The extent and terms of the guarantee are particularly important to them. It is your responsibility to make sure the risks are clearly explained and understood by these outside parties.

The way the bank wants to do the loan is not the way it always has to be. This is why your lawyer needs to see all the documents before you sign them. You need to decide what is of real importance to you getting the loan, personal pride, protecting non-business assets, whatever.

Make sure you can prepay the loan without penalty and that you pay interest only on the amount of money you actually borrow. You may want to negotiate a commitment fee up front in return for a lower rate on the borrowings. Perhaps you might want to negotiate a higher interest rate in return for a longer term on the note. Do not leave the final setting of the interest rate until the day of the loan closing. The bank lends you its depositors' money and pays interest to attract and retain these deposits. The bank needs to earn enough on its loans and investments to cover the interest paid to depositors and to pay all other operating costs of the bank and to earn a profit for the bank's owners.

As a borrower you can pay the bank directly with loan interest and you can, in addition, pay the bank indirectly by leaving non-interest earning money on deposit. This is called a compensating balance arrangement. Loan interest is a tax-deductible business expense; extra deposit balances are not. A lower stated interest rate on your loan because you are carrying compensating deposit balances might impress your business buddies and the cash looks good on your balance sheet, but you could be leaving too much on the table.

Your accountant can show you how to compare the true borrowing costs of the alternatives offered to you by the bank. The extra money you leave on deposit to get a lower loan rate might earn you more money than you save if it were invested in your business.

Banks use "loan pricing" formulae or models to figure out your interest rate. This approach is based upon earning a "target" rate of return on the loan portfolio. These loan pricing calculations can get fairly detailed. Some part of all deposits cannot be loaned or invested, but must be kept in the form of reserves. Different banks have different costs and different profit goals. And then, of course, a higher rate is charged to the higher risk loans.

The pricing of the loan, the interest rate to be charged on your loan, is part of the loan officer's presentation to the loan committee. The officer must justify and defend to the committee any loan rate that does not equal the target rate. So not only is a loan approved by the committee, but the interest is also approved by the committee.

If you leave final agreement on the interest rate until the loan closing, you may force the officer back into committee to get permission to make any changes. If you don't like the interest offered at closing, the loan won't close. The officer will look like a fool who can't negotiate with the borrower. You take the chance of having the committee, given a second look, refuse your loan entirely. Some borrowers let the interest rate become a matter of ego. They want to borrow at "prime." This is not a useful concern. I have seen deals collapse at the last minute over one-half of a percent. Getting the money is much more important than shaving the rate. I tell my clients, if your business can't carry a loan with at least a 20 percent interest rate you shouldn't be borrowing. Interest rates have been that high in the past and could be again. Also, you need to be earning a spread over the cost of the loan to make the borrowing profitable to you. Interest expense, included in your loan proposal cash flow projections, should be at a fair market rate. As a borrower, the best way to lower your interest rate is by lowering the bank's risk perception or risk rating of your loan.

Remember interest rates are negotiable. Make sure you establish that with your banker. Explain to the banker that when you make your payments on time and when the bank becomes more comfortable with your company's performance, you expect the rate charged to move downward.

Often, with notes running for more than a year or with loans secured by inventory and accounts receivable, the bank requires a signed loan agreement. This agreement can obligate the borrower to do a number of things: to provide regular financial reports to the bank, to maintain specified financial ratios, to obtain the bank's permission before selling assets, to provide insurance coverage, to allow the bank access to company books and records. This agreement can prohibit certain acts by the borrower such as selling the business, acquiring more fixed assets, entering into additional leases, borrowing more money, and paying management bonuses.

Loan agreements with these "positive" and "negative" covenants are becoming even more common. They start as "one-size-fits-all" lawyer boilerplate that has little relationship to how your business actually operates. Test the covenants out against your business. Could you have operated within them in the past three years? Can you observe them in the future? A common covenant, for example, requires the borrower to turn over to the bank 100 percent of the proceeds from the sale of assets pledged as collateral. This might not make sense for your business. What if you are regularly selling and replacing a pool of assets, like rental equipment, against which the bank has advanced a low percentage of loan to resale value?

The borrower may be required to submit a monthly report, signed by an officer of the company, called a Certificate of Compliance. This certificate states that the borrower is meeting the required ratios and target dollar amounts and is observing the other requirements outlined in the loan agreement. The loan can be called and payment demanded if the certificates are not submitted. Falsifying information on a certificate is considered fraud.

Make sure your internal accounting and reporting systems and your staff can produce the necessary information for the Certificate of Compliance by the required deadline. A borrower who is frequently late with the monthly compliance report or who submits inaccurate reports gets a lot of heat from the bank, is considered a higher risk borrower, and is creating the conditions to have the loan renewal turned down.

What is making the banker worry? Why are the covenants there? Ask the banker to sit down and explain to you how each of the loan covenants makes the loan a better loan for the bank. Once you understand the bank's true concerns and where it feels the need for protection, you can make suggestions. Then draw up an agreement that you understand, can live with, and that fits your situation. If later on you need to ask the bank to waive or release you from a loan agreement covenant, ask before you need it. Get the bank's waiver in writing. A bank is under no obligation to waive any of the terms of the loan agreement. If it does, it is usually a one-time waiver and does not change the basic terms of the original agreement.

A final review of the loan documents is your last chance to be certain that the source and timing of the loan repayment match the terms and maturity of the note. Don't sign the ninety-day note unless you intend to pay the loan in full at the end of ninety days. A verbal promise to renew your note is not binding on the bank. Never sign anything you do not clearly understand. Review all the documents ahead of time with your lawyer. Never rely on any verbal promises or statements. Recognize your borrowing needs in advance and plan your approach to the bank so you will have enough time to explore alternative sources and to negotiate proper terms and conditions.

Chapter 12
Planning the Renewal

So you have completed your loan, received your money, and can now forget about banking for a while. And if borrowing was an unpleasant experience, you plan to forget about banks for a long time.

Too bad. Borrowing does not work that way. Unless your loan was a very unusual one, you will either need to renew some portion of it in the future or you will need to borrow more money.

The smart business owner begins to prepare for the loan renewal or the next loan the day after the first loan is made. For most businesses bank borrowing is a major and continuing source of funds. Borrowing is not a deal; it should be a relationship, but some banks are treating it like a transaction.

The bank is under no obligation to renew your loan. If you don't have a pledge to renew in writing, you have nothing. And banks very rarely give out such written agreements. Whatever might have been discussed about renewing the loan was just that, discussion, not binding promises.

Things change. Economic, competitive, and technological forces are always at work. Credit quality rarely remains unchanged. Banks want the flexibility to get out of a loan situation they think might go bad. They want the flexibility to change loan policies or establish new credit criteria. You could be "invited" to move your loan to another lender at renewal. Or your later request for increased borrowings could trigger a turndown on the increase and an invitation to leave.

Surely banks don't really do such things? Yes, they do. The primary causes, both of which you can influence, are a deterioration in the borrower's credit worthiness and/or a loss of confidence in the borrower.

Your company may be falling short of the financial projections built into your cash flow statement or you may be showing too-rapid and unplanned growth. If, in addition, you have not kept the lender regularly informed of these significant problems, you have created the strong chance of your loan renewal being denied.

There are a number of positive actions you need to take and some things to avoid in building a sound and lasting borrowing relationship. View your borrowing as a selling or customer relationship. You are always selling your company to the bank. You try to create a personal as well as a business commitment on the part of your customers to buy from you. In the same way, try to build a personal as well as an institutional commitment on the part of the bank to keep lending to you.

Always tell the truth. Be open and honest. Nothing destroys trust faster than an uncovered lie, even a small one. Never surprise the banker with bad news. If you see some trouble for your business developing, keep the banker informed and up to date. This helps build confidence and gets the banker more on your team. Remember there is always someone looking over the banker's shoulder. It is very embarrassing for your lender to explain unexpected bad news to them.

Don't take your credit relationship for granted. Getting the first loan does not open the bank vault. There are borrowers who play "surprise blackmail." The lender gets a call. The borrower needs some more money for a vehicle or equipment or for inventory. They discuss it for a while. The lender says the bank will consider the additional money. The borrower says, "Consider fast. I already wrote the check."

The lender is in an uncomfortable position with two choices: get the loan approved quickly or return the check when it gets to the bank. If the check bounces will it hurt the borrower's business and perhaps endanger the loan already outstanding? A borrower might get away with this squeeze play once. Try it again and you can expect bouncing checks and a chill in the air.

Only make promises you intend to keep and keep all promises that you make. This helps maintain your credibility. The banker would rather have you tell him why a payment might be late than have you explain why a promised payment was not made.

Work at keeping the lines of communication open with your banker. You need to be constantly educating the banker about your business. Get your banker out to see your business at least once a year. Let him see that it is more than just a clean place. Introduce the bookkeeper or accountant. Show off some of your methods like approving new credit, monitoring and collecting customer account receivables, product quality controls, employee training programs and so on. This will help your loan officer be an informed advocate for your business in the credit approval process.

Get to know other people in the bank besides your loan officer, especially your loan officer's boss. When your officer is on vacation or out of the bank, be careful that you don't get too dependent on a secretary or administrative assistant. This person will not be your new loan officer if yours is promoted away or moves on, so ask to work with another loan officer or, best of all, with the likely successor to your present officer.

If your bank has receptions, stockholder meetings, seminars, workshops, etc., go from time to time and meet the other officers and directors. Get to know several layers of the bureaucracy. You want your name to be recognized by the members of the loan committee.

Refer other business to your bank, but be careful. Someone you refer to the bank indirectly represents you. If he is not of the highest quality, it can hurt your reputation by association. Don't refer weak companies and deadbeats.

Do you read your bank's annual report? Do you know what's important to its people and how they see themselves? Aren't these questions good salespeople ask about their customers?

Make sure you carefully follow any agreements you made regarding the level of balances to be kept in your bank accounts. These balances on deposit help raise the profitability of your loan to the bank and were taken into account in setting your loan interest rate.

It is necessary to meet all agreed-upon due dates for the delivery to the bank of financial statements, accounts receivable agings, inventory reports, and so on. This is all part of keeping the promises you have made. More importantly, the bank is interested in closely analyzing this information to detect any loan problems as soon as possible. The sooner a weakening credit is identified, the more choices the bank has to help the situation and to protect against loss. One text on problem loans lists eighty "early warning signs," organized into four categories: financial, management, operating, and banking. A borrower is rarely late with these reports when the results are good. Being late makes the banker think you are putting off bad news. Make a good impression: Have your statements and reports neat and accurate. You are dealing with a numbers-oriented person.

Your financial results will be compared to projections and budgets you included in your loan proposal. Set up your reports so this comparison can be easily seen. You gain credibility when you hit your projections or provide reasonable explanations for misses. It is a great investment of time to review your financials and other schedules with your bookkeeper before sending them to the bank. Then if your banker calls with any questions, you can answer them on the spot and build confidence and credibility with the bank.

Whether you like it or not, appearances count for a lot. Owner-managed businesses are seen as reflections of their owners. Turnover in your management team or accountant or lawyer is cause for some banker anxiety. A business lawsuit, losing a major customer, or having a key supplier put you on COD are significant to the bank. Divorces and other personal problems create uncertainty that your full attention is directed to the business. It is better that your banker hear about these kinds of problems from you and not from his boss, who reads it in the newspaper or hears it from another customer that morning.

Overdrawing your accounts and writing checks against uncollected funds are major irritants. Borrowers often mistakenly have an unconcerned attitude about managing their checking accounts. After all the overdrafts always get covered and few, if any, customer checks deposited have bounced.

The banker sees it differently. Shrinking bank deposits are one of the early warning signs of a business having problems. Overdrafts and drawing on uncollected funds are unauthorized loans and often interest-free. Would you like it if one of your customers came to your place of business and used some of your tools or equipment without your permission?

The banker is reluctant to bounce checks back because it can hurt the borrower's business reputation and perhaps indirectly endanger the ability to repay the loan. A daily list of depositors with overdrafts and uncollected funds is circulated within the bank. The borrower becomes known as a negative element to other bank officers. This carries over to the loan committee when the name comes up again. A regular appearance on these lists marks you as a sloppy businessperson and creates concern that other elements of your business are being mishandled as well.

Because of the way the check clearing system works, account officers must decide early in the business day whether to pay or to return checks that overdraw the account. Checks not returned by a mid-morning deadline must be paid. This can involve calls to the depositor to see if a mistake has been made, research into the account's overdraft history, and inspecting the checks to see who is going to get stuck with the return.

I never met a bank officer who liked running the daily overdraft report. It is a crummy and unproductive way to start your day, with pressure you really don't need. You do not have good feelings toward those customers who do this to you.

Worse than the overdraft list is the list of overdue loan interest and principal repayments—a bright red flag that the loan may be in trouble. This is a list of borrowers who have not kept their promise to the bank, and it is a list reviewed at the time of a bank examination. The examiners demand an explanation from the loan officers for every borrower of hers on the list. It may be no big deal to a borrower that his payment will be made a week late, after all his customers often pay late. It is a real big deal at the bank. Thanks to computers this lateness is noted and listed immediately and reviewed daily by senior level management.

Don't hide and make your loan officer call you to ask about late interest and principal payments. Call the officer before it happens with an explanation and tell him when you will make the payment. Then your loan officer will have the facts when his boss asks about your payment.

Appear on this list often enough or long enough and your loan will get you a special loan review. You don't want this to happen. Your loan could be downgraded. You will be asked to submit more reports on your business. You will be watched more closely. You could be asked to provide more collateral. You could be asked to move your loan to another bank.

And then there is the "technical exception" report on outstanding loans. It covers all the nitty gritty details built into keeping your borrowings in order. It shows such things as missing proof of insurance, missing signatures on guarantees, out-of-date personal financial statements, missing interim financials, needed corporate resolutions, and the like. Putting these items in order to the bank's satisfaction, once they have the money, is a very low priority for most borrowers. Technical exceptions in a loan portfolio is a job performance standard. Too many exceptions can cost the loan officer a raise. These exceptions are easily automated. So the system nags the officer endlessly to contact the borrower and get these details cleaned up. The borrower who does not cooperate with the loan officer is only hurting himself.

You will further lower the bank's level of confidence if you have speculative, unrelated and distracting business ventures on the side. Many balls in the air at the same time is a distraction. Most veteran loan officers can give you an example of a failed borrower who neglected the core business in pursuit of unrelated business or personal activities.

So you've been driving your banker crazy, and, unfortunately, it is now time to renew your note. The bank has lost confidence in your ability to repay the loan or dealing with you is not worth the effort. After all it is a seller's market. Here's the line we used:

"The bank has been reviewing its commitments to your type of loan and to your industry in particular. The bank's loan policy suggests that we have somewhat of an over-concentration of this type of asset. We feel it would be imprudent not to take this opportunity to seek a broader diversification of our loan portfolio. Consequently, we would like to suggest at this time that you move your borrowing relationship to another financial institution."

Let's hope you followed my earlier advice and developed a backup bank, because you need a new lender now.

The successful borrower knows that the selling never stops. You can not relax after the loan is made. You need to build a continuing relationship to assure renewal and availability of credit in the future. It is simply another task of management.

Chapter 13
Special Borrowing Situations

Small Business Administration Loans

The SBA has several business loan programs and something of an image problem with banks. In dealing with any SBA-related program the borrower must have time, patience, and persistence. If you are in a hurry and need money fast, it is usually better to try the pawn shop.

In part to escape its past reputation as the lender to the hopeless, the SBA has cut back on its direct loan programs to businesses. Three small loan programs are available, directed toward Vietnam and disabled veterans, the handicapped, and economic development projects. Your local SBA office will give you more details.

The SBA's major financing role now is as an insurer of loans made by others. The borrower deals directly with the bank, savings and loan, economic development agency, or direct SBA lender. The lender in turn approaches the SBA to guarantee this loan against failure to pay by the borrower. SBA guarantee insurance is used to offset or cover one weakness in what would otherwise be a satisfactory loan. The SBA helps when "financing on reasonable terms" is not available locally. For example, SBA-insured real estate loans for owner-occupied commercial property are one of the very few sources of long-term financing for the smaller business.

Or perhaps the company needs five years to repay an equipment loan, but the bank normally only lends for three years. Perhaps everything is good but there is insufficient collateral to satisfy the bank's desire for a secondary source of repayment. Perhaps the company is new and has not had time to build a track record satisfactory to the bank.

If your business loan application is turned down by a lender and the reason for the turndown seems to be one of those just described, you might want to try for an SBA-insured loan.

At the present time the SBA will insure up to 90 percent of some loans and provide maximum insurance of $750,000 on one borrower. If the loan is not repaid the SBA pays off the insured portion to the original lender. This doesn't erase or forgive the borrower's loan. The loan still exists, but now is owed directly to the SBA. The SBA can do everything to collect the loan that the original lender could do: seize collateral, get legal judgments, or make guarantors pay.

SBA-guaranteed loans tend to be smaller loans that require additional time and work from the bank officer. SBA-imposed ceilings on points, closing costs, and interest rates make these insured loans less costly to the borrower and less profitable to the lender. Many banks and savings and loans want nothing to do with SBA loans, but won't tell you this fact. No bank likes to state publicly its refusal to cooperate with the government in helping small business. If you think your loan might require SBA insurance, you are wasting your time at these places. If your loan officer has never done an SBA loan before, you are guaranteed a long and frustrating experience.

Call your local SBA office and get the names of the financial institutions in your city that are making SBA-guaranteed loans. Ask specifically for the Certified Lenders or the Preferred Lenders. Certified lenders are mostly banks that do a lot of SBA lending. They handle much of the application review and processing, but still need a final approval from the SBA. The SBA promises an answer within three business days. Preferred lenders can respond even more quickly. Get the name of the loan officer at each of these places who does the SBA-related work and see only that officer. Often only one officer at a particular bank is either assigned SBA loan responsibility or develops a personal interest in these loans.

SBA loans are certainly not automatic. The SBA district loan officers make an independent credit judgment. An SBA loan application package completed by the proposed borrower and the non-SBA lender's analysis are part of their review. The cooperative working relationship between the SBA loan officers and the local lenders varies from community to community. In some places it is outright hostile. Other areas have a history of cooperation. It depends upon the personalities of the individuals involved, the level of local loan demand, and the distrust one type of bureaucrat has for another.

The SBA can name successful companies that were started with guaranteed loans. There is no reason not to try the program if it can help your company.

Borrowing at a Bank in Trouble

Until recently bank failures were most often caused by internal fraud rather than by external economic conditions. Deregulation permitted a combination of unsound lending practices, greed, poor judgment, and weak economic conditions to collapse banks.

It doesn't take much effort to know if your lending bank is failing or experiencing weak earnings. Your local newspaper probably reports the ratings compiled by one of the private bank rating services. Banks publish quarterly financial results and, of course, people talk to each other.

Trying to turn a money-losing bank around is like trying to U-turn an aircraft carrier. There is a lot of momentum to be reversed. The bank concentrates on fixing the problem loans. Moreover, even the quality borrower comes under closer review because the bank fears more losses. Lower-quality borrowers will feel pressure either to upgrade their loans with more collateral and financial reporting or to move their loans to other lenders.

At the bank, simple daily administrative details, like mailing out statements or returning phone calls, are neglected. Documents, files, letters, contracts are missing or misfiled. There is a high degree of loan officer turnover and account re-assignment. It becomes almost impossible for current borrowers to get additional credit. New policies and procedures are set up and there is a fear of making mistakes. Everything takes much longer as more people are consulted in every decision. Tempers are shorter and personnel less accommodating and more rule-bound.

My advice for top-quality borrowers is to move to a sounder bank. You do not need the inevitable delay, paralysis, and inconvenience that sets into a troubled bank. If you cannot easily move your loan to another bank, you should avoid drawing attention to yourself while you try to set up a move. The squeaky wheel gets the grease and the obvious weak credit gets attention first.

So don't be obvious. Don't overdraw your checking accounts. Don't be late with any loan payments. Don't be late with any promised financial statements or reports. Return the banker's phone calls promptly. Be pleasant, upbeat, and friendly when you are in the bank. You want to be a pleasant non-problem. Like the swimming duck you want to be tranquil and serene on the surface and paddling like crazy out of sight as you work to line up another lender.

If your bank is closed and sold to a new bank your loan will be in one of three conditions: It will be purchased from the Federal Deposit Insurance Corporation at 100 percent of the amount owed by the new bank, and you will be a customer of the new bank. This is probably all right except you had no say in choosing your lender. Your new bank may have no experience in your industry. Its loan policies could give low priority to your type of business. You have to sell yourself all over again.

Or your loan will have been purchased by the new bank from the FDIC at some discount from the amount owed. All of the above negatives still apply and you are in the doghouse, labeled a weak, low-quality credit. Remember the new owners were not willing to pay one hundred cents on the dollar to own your loan. This discount purchase does not, however, change the amount you owe. If you owed $20,000 before the bank failure, then you owe $20,000 after the takeover. The new bank wants to shape you up or ship you out. It will be anxious to restructure your loan to their standards. They might also cut you a deal if you can move your loan to another bank. A simple example: you originally made a $100,000 loan secured by real estate. Land values have declined. Your collateral today would support a loan of $75,000. The new bank bought your loan for $65,000. If you could borrow the money elsewhere, don't you think they would let you pay off the loan in full with $75,000? These kinds of deals can be done. A lot depends on the attitude of the new bank and the personalities of the people involved.

The third likelihood is that you will owe the full amount to the FDIC. The FDIC is a liquidator, not a lender. It wants to collect on your loan. The Feds can be very tough. You have a problem, since you were declared either unfit or simply unwanted by the takeover bank. But again deals can be done. If you can offer the FDIC a better deal than they think they can get through liquidation and collection efforts, you may be able to settle your debt at a substantial discount.

A failing bank creates problems for the quality borrower. It also creates opportunities for some weaker borrowers. The weakest borrowers, unable to strike a deal with the FDIC, are almost certain to be liquidated.

The Bothersome Small Loan

It is easier to borrow larger rather than smaller amounts. The small business, especially the first-time borrower, that needs a small loan finds it hard to interest lenders in its request.

What is a small loan? It all depends on which bank you ask. To a major East Coast Money Center bank less than $500,000 could be a "small" loan. To your independent neighborhood bank loans under $50,000 might be small. When your business loan needs are about what it would cost to buy an upscale car, you are clearly a small loan.

When your competition for the lender's attention are married DINKS (Dual Income/No Kids) buying a Beamer (BMW auto) you have a problem. The banker would prefer to make the car loan. The automobile is almost certain to be better as collateral than what your business has to offer. The household income available to service the car loan is probably more dependable than your self-employment income. The car owner could probably get a second job to keep the payments up. The small businessperson is already working sixty hours a week.

Processing a car loan requires filling out a loan application and making a credit check. Making a business loan requires much more interview time, analyzing financial statements, and visiting your place of business. It requires checking business and personal credit history, more complicated documents, and understanding your business strengths and weaknesses. From the banker's point of view, making a $25,000 business loan to a new borrower takes as much time and effort as making a $100,000 business loan, and a lot more effort than a $25,000 car loan. The car loan is less risky and more profitable to the bank.

You can improve your chances of getting your small loan approved. Take it seriously and prepare your presentation as if you were needing millions instead of thousands. Make the "mechanical" elements of the loan so clear and easy that you require minimal brainpower on the part of the loan officer.

Have neat and organized business and personal financial statements and be sure to include copies of your tax returns for the past three years.

Provide equipment and other asset lists with date purchased, original cost, and estimate of current value. Attach a list of customers and business references and include their addresses and phone numbers, etc.

Expect to pay a high interest rate. The bank will want you to keep all your business and personal deposit accounts with it. Short of cash, your vehicle is the preferred collateral. If possible, interest the banker in the future of your business, its growth and your potential to be a larger and more profitable customer of the bank.

Ask for as short a repayment period as you can comfortably handle. Accept credit life and disability insurance on the loan, if suggested by the banker. This is somewhat costly insurance for larger loans, but it makes the small loan more profitable to the bank.

Some of my business friends claim they get a better response if they ask for a personal vacation loan on an installment basis. The banker treats it like a personal loan and seems less interested in digging into the business. Don't ask for an amount larger than what you really need. It is an old trick and doesn't work. Some business owners find it easy to get several personal credit cards and use the cash advance feature as a small revolving line of credit.

Once you have established yourself as a dependable borrower, the small loan becomes easier and is often done over the phone and by mail.

Handling the Loan Turndown

When you go through all efforts of a loan proposal and properly select the bank and the banker, you are still not guaranteed a positive answer.

A good credit officer will quickly turn down loan applications that are an obvious waste of time: a poor payment history on prior loans, a purpose not acceptable to bank policy, already too much debt in the company, unprofitable operations, or no collateral.

What about those loans where you, the borrower, are surprised at the turndown? What should you do?

The decision to deny credit can be easy, but actually telling another person his business is not acceptable to your bank is hard to do. After all, even though it is a business proposition, no one likes to deliver bad news or disappoint someone. Some officers have standard form letters because they don't want to get in a heated discussion with a disappointed business owner over the phone. Others make a phone call, but try to keep the conversation quite short and vague and blame some faceless loan committee.

It is almost impossible to get a "No" decision turned into a "Yes." You are asking the lender to admit to a mistake, to admit that he was wrong to turn you down. People do not like to admit mistakes.

Suppose it is your fault. You discover, after the turndown, a significant error in your historical financials or in your projections. These errors made your finances look worse than they really are. Will the bank change its mind? Probably not. After all you have just demonstrated an inability to provide accurate information.

What if you discover the loan officer simply did not understand a significant part of your presentation. Will he change his mind? Probably not. After all you are now proven to be a poor communicator.

If you persist in trying to reverse the decision, then present a meaningfully different and new proposal. Then you are saying to the bank, "Look I took your advice. I rethought my plans. I now have a better way. Please look at my new and different proposal."

In reality, your loan may just not be of bank quality. Maybe another kind of lender might be interested. You simply cannot allow the turndown to go unexplained if you do not understand the reason behind it.

It is the rare loan officer who will volunteer to give you the help you want: a personal meeting with a detailed explanation of the turndown and some guidance on how to qualify for a loan. If you meet such an individual, make a note of his name. He is likely to be a quality individual whom you want as a loan officer at a later date. The bank has a lot of reasons for not wanting this meeting. The officer has already spent time on a loan that went nowhere. If your loan was turned down in the loan committee, it has already caused the officer some personal embarrassment. The borrower will generally be angry and will try to make the bank admit it was wrong to deny credit. Last, the bank could be spending time helping you move your relationship to a competitor.

But you need this meeting. Perhaps there is something not understood that, if corrected, would incline the bank to change the decision. If you are truly not credit worthy, you need to know that. Why waste time looking for a loan when it can't be had? Best of all maybe you can learn something that will help you get a positive response from another bank.

Maybe you need to approach a more specialized kind of lender, like a commercial finance company.

So wait a day or two after the turndown. Then call your loan officer and ask for a meeting to review your loan proposal and your company's credit worthiness. Be clear that you are not asking the banker to change the decision. Indicate you respect their opinion and appreciate the time they spent on giving your request consideration. Tell them you need their advice. You want to understand their reasoning and learn what changes need to be made in your company so you can eventually qualify for bank credit. Make no threats. Be calm and don't tell them that you are going to apply for a loan at another lender.

The chances are little better than even that you will get the meeting. If the bank refuses to meet with you, it is saying you have no future with them. It doesn't want your business.

If you are able to set up the meeting, remember that your purpose is to ask questions and to learn all you can about the credit weaknesses the bank sees in either your company or in your loan presentation. Don't argue. Don't object. Ask questions about factual matters. Your goal is to learn what steps need to be taken to make your company credit worthy. You want to benefit from the banker's objective view of your company and broader experience. You want to get these people who told you "No" to advise you on what it takes to get a "Yes" from someone else.

Lending is not scientifically accurate. The solution could be as simple as finding another lender more familiar with your industry or more willing to take risk. Perhaps there are some holes in your information. Maybe you can rework your business plans and come up with a more satisfactory proposal. Perhaps the only answer is more investment, not more debt. Or maybe you need to improve the profitability of your company, manage its cash flow and current assets more efficiently, or lease rather than buy new equipment. Whatever it is, you need to know about it.

A meeting like this takes a lot of patience and self-control on the part of the borrower. It is more productive than staying angry or submitting the same loan proposal again and again to different lenders.

Ideas for the Loan in Trouble

For whatever reason, your company cannot make your loan payments as agreed. You have kept your loan officer informed of your circumstances, but that isn't solving the problem.

This continues for a while, falling behind, catching up, falling behind until you are now ninety days late with an interest payment.

Before you fell the full ninety days behind your loan was probably put on the banks internal "Watch List." This is a list of borrowers whose payment record is spotty or whose collateral may have had a large decline in value. For example, loans secured by real estate in a falling real estate market often make it to the Watch List. Top management of the bank is now aware of your condition as a problem loan. Your loan is being closely monitored, and your loan officer's handling of the situation is being watched. Your loan officer will have to answer a lot of questions about the loan, about you, your company, and your industry. The officer will want to talk to you more frequently. If you don't return phone calls, if you go into hiding, your officer can neither explain nor defend your situation to the regulators and bank management.

The bank's loan review area will now make a new evaluation of your loan quality, your credit file, and all documents associated with your loan. Your loan officer will ask for a new set of company financial statements and new personal financial statements from you and any other individuals signing on or guaranteeing the loan. The officer will be particularly careful to get the borrower/guarantors to sign the new set of financial statements.

On these new financials borrowers are tempted to do a little creative accounting by concealing or overvaluing assets and by understating or concealing other debt. Presenting financial statements that are not true is an act of fraud. There is no place to hide when you are caught. Fraud wipes out many legal defenses you might want to use later in a lawsuit against the bank. Fraud can cost you the protection of the bankruptcy laws.

At the ninety day point, with few exceptions, regulations require the bank to put your loan on a non-accrual basis. This means from an accounting standpoint the bank may no longer count as income earned the interest you owe but have not paid. If your monthly loan interest cost is $1,000, the bank's monthly income has been cut by that amount.

When a loan is placed on non-accrual, some borrowers mistakenly believe that the bank is forgiving the interest. This is not correct. Nothing is forgiven. All that is owed and unpaid is still owed.

All interest and principal to be paid in the future is still owed and payment is expected. The bank still hopes the loan might recover, interest payments will begin again, and the loan need not be charged off.

But the clock is really ticking and pressure on the bank and on your loan officer increases. The next required step is to charge off a portion or all of your loan. A charge-off reduces the value of your loan shown on the bank's books. Charging off or writing off the loan in no way forgives or reduces the amount you owe the bank. It is an internal bank procedure. And the full amount of your loan continues to pile up owed but unpaid interest. The charge-off marks down the loan to the bank's estimate of net value it would receive after foreclosure on the loan, liquidation of collateral, and related legal and liquidation expenses. Charge-offs are a current expense to the bank, reduce its earnings, and weaken its capital base. Charge-offs draw the attention of the regulators. Banks hate to have charge-offs.

Banks, like elephants, never forget. They will not just walk away from a loan and forget it. They might not bother the borrower for a while, perhaps as long as four years, but they have neither forgiven nor forgotten. Only a discharge in bankruptcy or an agreement negotiated between the bank and the borrower will stop a bank from trying to collect on a loan.

Usually by the time your loan is sixty days past due, but certainly by the time it goes on non-accrual, the bank has come up with a preliminary approach to your problem loan. In the best of worlds you and the bank might decide to work together and restructure the loan. They might lower the interest rate or extend the time to pay or even lend you more money. As part of these early negotiations the bank often will want the borrower to promise that if the situation does not improve, the borrower will peaceably allow the liquidation of the collateral or of the company. Be certain that you can keep these promises and live with the results.

At the other extreme, your loan will be declared immediately due and payable in full. If you cannot pay the loan or refinance it elsewhere, the bank will move to foreclosure. Collateral is taken and sold. Guarantors on the loan will be required to make up any shortages between collateral proceeds and the amount owed.

The approach taken by the bank will depend on how the loan officers see the situation. Most important is their experience with you and their evaluation of your character and management abilities. Have you kept your promises in the past? Have you stayed in communication with the bank? Is the loan a problem because of your lack of management ability or because of larger problems within your company's industry? Do you have a plan for pulling out of the situation? Are you just blindly hanging on and hoping for a lucky break?

The borrower who looks to the bank for a lot of help in putting together a business turnaround plan will be disappointed. The possible legal liabilities coming from taking an active role in your business are too high for the bank. The bank probably does have some thoughts on how to improve your business and work out of the situation, but the officer will mostly hold back and respond only to your suggestions and ideas.

The bank's major concern is getting the loan repaid. The borrower must make a strong case that demanding immediate repayment will produce the largest loss to the bank. A written plan of action and detailed cash flow projections are the documents required to buy time and patience from the bank.

It must be a reasonable plan for the bank to take the position that the present loss will not get worse but will, in fact, diminish in some foreseeable time frame. In the lender's mind there is always the question, "Does the borrower understand the business problems? Can he correct these problems in time?" Nothing will make the bank turn out the lights faster than a loss of confidence in the borrower.

The next factors in importance are the value and quality of the loan collateral. If there is a lot of collateral that will hold its value, the bank can be more patient. If collateral is accounts receivable in an unprofitable business with declining sales, the bank will want to move rapidly.

The bank considers some of its own financial issues, such as the size of its reserve for loan losses and current and expected profits. The bank is concerned about the impact of a new charge-off on its own financial ratios. The regulators closely watch these indicators as a sign of a bank's financial health.

It is very tempting for a bank with a well collateralized non-performing loan to call the loan and sell the collateral. It saves future time and expense in working with the borrower and makes the bank's ratios look better to the regulators.

The bank will determine whether it has any legal weaknesses in its loan documents that might prevent it from collecting the loan and let the borrower off the hook. The bank's internal review will decide if the conduct of your loan officer has in any way given you reason to sue the bank and stop the collection efforts.

Likewise you and your attorney will need to meet and decide on a plan for working with the bank. Don't be in a hurry to get your attorney directly involved with the bank. Attorneys are more often trained as fighters, not negotiators. They can heat up a situation real fast. Showing up with your attorney will likely draw out the bank's attorney. This can take away some negotiating flexibility from the loan officer. It is harder to back away from positions arrived at with attorneys present. The potential for conflict moves to a higher and more intense level. Even when holding your attorney in the background, sign nothing without her review.

Borrowers should always keep copies of everything that they have signed. This is never the time for "handshake deals." Never sign anything blank. Never leave a lender's office without having copies of documents that you signed during that meeting. If, later, your attorney needs to review the loan documentation, you are in a difficult situation. Having to ask the lender for copies gives him some psychological power over you. It permits him to delay and irritate you.

If you are unable to provide your attorney with copies of all bank documents, it is difficult for your attorney to determine the true extent of any weaknesses in your or the bank's position.

You should be very cautious if your lender requests the loan papers and collateral documents be redone and resigned. This "re-papering" of the entire deal can be an effort to close some existing holes in the lender's legal position. This request is frequently the last chance for the borrower to renegotiate the loan or win some concessions from the bank. In turn, the borrower usually gives up the right to sue the bank for any prior errors and permits the bank to perfect its rights to the collateral.

Make sure that from the very beginning you understand all your legal options to include both business and personal bankruptcy. There is no need to threaten the lender with the possibility of taking your company into bankruptcy. She knows all about it and doesn't like to hear about it any more than is necessary.

It is easy for the business owner, sincerely trying to work out the loan in trouble, to get very frustrated with the situation. It takes an incredible amount of patience, self-control, and energy to work with the bank and to keep your business going at the same time.

The process of working out what to do with your loan can move rather swiftly or it can drag on for many months. Some banks will move your loan to more experienced loan work-out or "special asset" officers. The borrower must then learn to work with a new set of opponents. Special asset officers can have more bargaining power than the loan officer. They will want to pick up the pace and get the case closed. Changes in bank ownership usually bring new teams of people with new attitudes and a get-tough policy for troubled borrowers.

Your best outcome is a restructured loan your business can live with. The bank's best outcome is collecting more on the loan from a continuing business than from a business liquidation. At some point it will all end. Either you will have negotiated a new deal or the bank will be closing out the loan and your business.

Your Business Is Growing

Your business is succeeding. You are selling more and getting new customers. Why isn't the banker smiling?

If growth is good, why is it of particular concern to a banker? A banker with any miles on him at all can remember some good loans that went bad when the borrower was unable to manage the growth of the company. The company grew right into failure. You can have too much of a good thing!

Only about 8 percent of all companies ever reach two milestones: surviving for more than ten years and growing to at least twenty employees. Growth can strain the management skills of the business owner. There are lots of questions. Is there a management team in place or is it a solo show? Will management delegate? Will management departmentalize? Are the employees trained and capable of operating at a larger scale? Will quality, customer service, cost control, or internal procedures deteriorate under pressure to take care of new customers and higher demand? Is growth being managed or is it just happening?

Growth almost always strains the cash resources of the company. Will profit margins slip at a time when profits are needed most in the business? In most cases growth requires additional fixed assets or additional inventory or accounts receivable. It is said that half the companies that fail are profitable in an accounting sense; they just ran out of cash and borrowing power to pay their bills.

If you are in a growth pattern the banker is particularly concerned about the existence of sound operational and financial controls and about the depth and balance of your management team. You won't impress the banker with hype, glitz, and a super sales growth story. In fact, that should be the last thing you try. It is hard for the enthusiastic charged-up businessperson, whose hard work is paying off, to approach the loan request in a "buttoned-up" fashion. Fight the urge to cheer and smile. Recognize up front exactly what concerns the bank. Show from the start why your team will be able to grow the company safely.

Frequently the bank's agreement to lend will be conditional upon additional equity coming into the company first. The concern for a safety cushion of equity rises with the growth curve of your business.

An uncontrolled growth situation that requires more loans will put the banker in the dilemma of lending more money into an already risky situation or shutting down a "promising" company.

Detailed and well-supported financial projections are most critical to the success of your loan request. Show how you plan to build earnings, monitor profitability, check out new credit sales, control product quality, and establish multiple supply sources.

The bank wants regular financial and operating reports so it can track your actual performance against your initial projections. It will want to see you in person, often. It wants to believe it has some control over the situation and can exit the loan if it wants.

There is a twist to an old saying, "When the sun is shining the banker knows it will rain."

Borrowing to Start a New Business

I tell people thinking about going into business for themselves that no one will ever love their dream as much as they do: not their friends, not their spouse, not their mother, and certainly not the banker.

Incredible amounts of time are wasted by start-ups trying to borrow money from a bank. This is where the realities of business really hit home to the fledgling company. No one likes lending to a start-up. I don't think it matters much whether seven out of ten or six out of ten businesses are no longer in existence after five years. Let the researchers argue the point. The odds of survival are low. Of course, the new businessperson believes she will be one of the three or four survivors. No one starts a business planning to fail, although many fail to plan.

It matters not to the bank that probably no more than two out of the six or seven disappear with a loss to their creditors. When you are lending depositors' money you need to be repaid by all your borrowers, not by just 80 to 90 percent. At some banks the loan policy does not even permit loans to start-ups.

From time to time, start-up businesses do manage to borrow from banks. A survey by *INC* magazine of successful companies revealed that 30 percent of them had obtained some start-up money from banks. From this I figure that your chances of getting a start-up loan from a bank are less than one in ten. Since the average company in this survey started with total capital of $34,000, the banks don't look too adventurous.

What's the secret? You almost don't have to need the money. The successful start-up borrower is probably a business selling to other businesses. It is most likely a business with a tangible product, either a manufacturer or a wholesaler. The deal has to be stronger than moose breath. There is a lot of owner's or stockholders' money in the company. The bank is probably advancing less than 30 percent of the total funds needed. Ideally, the bank's money is "last in." It is not advanced to the company until after the business is up and running. The bank has collateral of current assets, accounts receivable and inventory, the owner's personal guarantee, and anything else they can get their hands on.

The management has meaningful prior experience in this or a similar line of business (they aren't opening a restaurant just because their neighbors tell them they are good cooks) and is already known to the bank. Above all there is a written business plan, a heavyweight, detailed, well-thought-out business plan that can stand up under microscopic examination.

Don't spend your time pointlessly running from bank to bank collecting loan denials. Instead, do like most business start-ups. Scrape together all your personal assets. Write a business plan to convince friends, neighbors, family, and business contacts that you have what it takes to succeed with their money not the bank's.

Borrowing to Buy an Existing Business

What could be easier? You have found an operating, profitable-appearing business that you can buy. All you need do is borrow some money from the bank and it is yours. The company will literally pay for itself.

We read about companies being bought every day. It's a whole new industry. It even has a catchy name: "LBO" or "Leveraged Buy Out." You use the assets of the company that you are buying as collateral for the purchase loan. Surely the bank will see what a good deal this is and lend you the money.

Yes, the bank is more interested in this kind of a loan than in a start-up business loan. But to stand out from all the other eager buyers who show up at the bank, do your homework before your first visit with the lender. Besides the basic seven questions asked of any borrower, here are some more.

First, why is the business for sale? Is there some threat or problem that the present owner is trying to escape? A new highway? A rent increase? New competitors and technology? Worn out equipment and vehicles? Unionization? Is it one of these negative reasons or is it simply retirement time, boredom, or necessitated by a divorce? If the seller's motives are negative, then how do you plan to handle these problems?

Second, do you have a lawyer representing you and reviewing the sales contract? Never mind the business broker who represents the seller. The bank will want to see the contract. It is concerned about hidden liabilities cropping up after the purchase and perhaps endangering the repayment program or the collateral position.

Third, buying a business should be approached like buying a used car. Have you or your accountant done "due diligence" on the company? Figures don't lie, but liars figure. This means assume the seller is a rascal. Now where would he have buried the bad news and created the false good news?

Have you reviewed the financial statements in detail? Don't rely on numbers prepared by the business broker. Are the sales truly as represented? Is there a large contract about to expire? Is the business depending heavily on one or two major customers? How much of the inventory is stale and overvalued? Are the receivables really collectable? There are lots more questions.

Fourth is "goodwill," the difference between the purchase price and the true value of the assets you are buying, a big part of the price? Banks won't finance goodwill. Since banks won't lend full value of the collateral, your down payment will be at least the sum of the goodwill plus the discount or loan margin on the collateral.

Fifth, do you know anything about running the business you are buying? Capacity and all of the "C" questions from Chapter 9 will apply. Will the present owner cash out completely and ride into the sunset? The bank would prefer that the seller stay available to show you the ropes. It would be even happier if the seller showed confidence in the business by financing part of the purchase, subordinate to the bank debt, on a long-term basis.

Sixth, have you prepared balance sheet, income statement, and cash flow projections for the company showing the interest and principal impact of the buyout loan and any other expense and income changes you plan to make? Your accountant or consultant who helped you with the due diligence tire-kicking should work with you to complete these projections.

If your target company is already a bank borrower, you have a choice to make. Start with the seller's bank or your bank? I would prefer that you start with your own bank, especially if you are already a well-established borrower. It is unlikely that your bank will contact the seller's bank for details on the seller's company. It is certain that the seller's bank will contact your bank about your credit and character.

Why does it matter? I would rather be turned down by my bank and still have the option to approach the seller's bank than the reverse. In theory, at least, the seller's bank knows most about the target company. Assume the seller's bank turns down the loan. Then, when I approach my own bank, it will be even more suspicious of the quality of the intended purchase. If my bank turns me down first, I can still approach the seller's bank. They might see me as a better risk than their present borrower.

Borrowing to Buy a Franchise

A nice fact about franchises is that bankers know they are less risky than an independent start-up. It would be a rare bank whose loan policy prohibits lending to franchises. In other words you can get an appointment at the bank to talk about a franchise loan.

Franchises have several significant attractions from a banker's point of view. The loans tend to be larger or of an "efficient" size. There is a business plan, checklists of operating procedures, site selection help, training for the franchisee, and established name and product recognition. There is a franchisor who has a financial interest in your success, a track record of similar operations, some fixed assets (although often specialized), and usually a substantial real financial commitment on your part required by the franchisor.

Still, you will have to persuade the bank that the franchisor's business concept, operational support and training, along with your experience and ability, will be winners. A good way to make your case is to spend time customizing and tying the franchisor's package into your local marketplace. Verify the expense estimates with franchisees already in operation and modify them to reflect your local market wage rates and construction costs. Expand the advertising budget into a suggested schedule of ads in local media with perhaps some rough versions of the ads. Do surveys to show there is a need in the local market for the franchise product or services.

Now not all franchises are created equal. The banks prefer lending to the franchisees of the larger, older, well-established operations. If you are the first operator of a particular franchise in your town, especially if it is not a national name, you will have to break some new ground. Come prepared to show success stories in similar communities and markets. Talk to your fellow franchise operators in other towns and find out where they bank. Then refer your local bank to these out-of-town banks for more background on the performance of the franchise.

Not all franchisors provide a high level of franchisee support. Some make money on selling franchises, not from royalties or from selling product or services to their franchisees. The bank will want to check out the reputation of the franchisor and will need a copy of the franchisor's disclosure statements.

Once, on a thin deal, I refused to lend to a would-be-franchisee because the franchisor was not following the required information disclosure rules. Right or wrong, I figured if the franchisor wouldn't do it right on the front end, they wouldn't be there later on, if the franchisee/borrower needed them.

Sometimes what the borrower thinks is a franchise is not. It is a business opportunity with much less territorial protection, less operational support, less national advertising, and a lot less of everything, including bank attention. You really damage your credibility if you start talking about financing for a franchise that turns out to be a business opportunity.

Banks spend a lot of time evaluating the franchisee's capacity. Do you have the high level of energy and motivation necessary to put in the long hours at the store? Some people mistakenly believe that the right franchise name guarantees success and an easy life. Is the franchisee able to work within the company system and follow the basic operating procedures? The bank is looking for the right blend of drive, motivation, and a willingness to follow guidelines. Be sure your resume shows these personal traits. Successful franchisees are often refugees from larger companies who are fed up with working to make someone else wealthy.

The reputation of the franchisor, the experience of other franchisees, the completeness of your financial assumptions, the quality of your local market research, and the depth of your financial and emotional commitment must all come together in a persuasive presentation.

Chapter 14
Summary Review

This chapter is a highly condensed, comprehensive summary of the first thirteen chapters. It is intended for those of you who read this book in bits and pieces when you could take time away from your business.

Reading this chapter now will help you pull together all the previous material and focus on what it takes to win the battle for the banker's "Yes."

If you managed to read this book straight through or at least relatively uninterrupted, you probably can skip to the end of this chapter and read "A Final Thought or Two."

In six months or a year from now you can come back to this chapter and quickly review the book's key points.

There are many businesses that want to borrow money. From the banker's point of view there are too few qualified borrowers. Lenders have to sort through a lot to find the deals that fit the needs and policies of their bank.

Borrowed money has four uses: to buy assets, to replace other loans or credit, to replace an equity investment, or to pay for expenses needed to create new revenue.

There are only four ways to repay a loan: with another loan, by liquidating or selling off assets, by additional equity investment in the company, or with excess cash flow from profitable operations.

Banks like to make productive loans. Loans that result in increased sales, stronger cash flow, and higher profits.

Even all the bankable loans do not get made. Most often the loan proposal doesn't make a very good first impression. It is incomplete, requiring too much research, analysis, and investigation for the dollar amount requested.

To get a loan you must distinguish yourself from the crowd. You must convince the loan officer that you are different from the "typical" unprofessional and unprepared businessman.

The borrowing experience is not an even match. The borrower deals with lenders only infrequently, but the lender deals all the time with borrowers.

Borrowers do not know how to present themselves to their best advantage in a game they play infrequently. They often take what they can get and don't get what they need.

Getting a loan is like making a sale. You cannot make a sale if you do not understand the buyer's needs, motivation, and limits. You need to understand the pressures placed upon the banks and why they act the way they do.

Banks are safekeeping warehouses for depositors' money. This role is so important that the government taxes the banks to set up a deposit insurance fund run by the Federal Deposit Insurance Corporation.

Government supervisors regulate banks for the safety of the depositor with less than $100,000 in the bank. No government regulator looks out for the business borrower.

Everyone in a bank has a boss or some other authority or monitor looking over his shoulder. The loan officer is constantly second-guessed by the system. And then the regulators come to visit for their required exams and review everyone else's reviews. It is amazing that anything gets done at all.

In addition to these on-site inspections, the regulators require banks to submit a number of periodic financial condition reports, to maintain various dollar reserves for possible loan and security losses, and to maintain specific financial performance ratios.

The agency which insures banks comes in direct contact with borrowers only after it has taken over a failing bank. It wants to collect all the weak loans and sell all the healthy loans to another bank. They take a tough attitude toward borrowers.

The pressure is on the banks not only to make good quality new loans, but also to reduce the level of risk already on their books. Banks want to shift weaker and troublesome-appearing loans out of the bank, before they become a serious problem.

For borrowers a back up bank is a necessity. A bank's willingness and ability to lend can change with new management, with new ownership, with changes in the bank's financial health, and with local economic or industrial activity.

Is your loan officer hung up on the bank's rules? Is he inflexible? Does everything seem to take too long? The answer to all of these may be yes, but it is unlikely that you can change it. As problem loans batter the banking industry, your banker has shown an increased interest in your company. This is self-protective behavior. The bankers have become information addicts with a very high need for written information about your company.

Increasingly adversarial customers, attorneys, and juries have made bankers super cautious about what they tell their customers and what business advice they may give. Now the loan officer is very careful about giving friendly advice and sharing business information.

The major change in banking in the past generation is simply the loss of a very predictable, stable, and controlled operating environment. The opportunity to make an error has never been greater. The consequences of an error have never been more severe.

The banking industry's response to this unstable environment is to interview and investigate the potential borrower more carefully. More time and effort are spent on cross-checking an applicant's background, personal and business references, and on thoroughly searching public records.

Always give yourself lots of lead time when you want something from the bank. Start all major transactions weeks ahead of your due date. You want to deal as high up in the bank's power structure as you can. Deal with someone who has the internal clout to make an exception to "bank policy" once in a while for your benefit and get away with it.

The bankers' main concern is that their depositors' money, lent to businesses, is repaid.

Banks manage company credit risk by a thorough evaluation of your loan application, through the bank's credit decision process, and by continuing to track the borrower's performance after the loan is made. Industry risk and company risk come together in the lending process in a technique called "comparative analysis." Your company's financial structure and performance are compared to composite statistics of other companies in your industry.

Figure out why your company is different from the bank's composite for your industry. Are they bad reasons or good reasons? Also get any comparative statistics available through your industry associations or trade groups. Make the same kind of analysis and response.

The bank's analysis starts in the credit department, where your carefully prepared loan presentation is placed in the hands of a recent college or business school graduate. The trainee then puts your financials into the bank's standard analytical format, orders credit reports, and does other "grunt work."

Smaller banks hire people away from bigger banks. This makes for consistency in the approach to business credit within the banking community. So regardless of the size of your bank, the effort you give to your loan proposal should be the same.

Your loan officer, depending upon how many borrowers he is assigned, may leave much of the numbers analysis to the credit department. It will be the loan officer who carries the ball to get your loan approved. Ask and understand, before you ever have to borrow, how loan authority is allocated at your bank.

Ask about the officer's lending authority. If his loan authority is less than what you need to borrow, then you may be facing delays waiting for his boss or the loan committee to meet. Ask how long you should expect the bank to take in responding to a loan request.

Some loan officers turn down a borrower on their own and then say that the loan committee shot them down. This is pretty sleazy, but saves arguments. Knowing ahead of time what size loan must go to committee will cut out this nonsense.

A key subjective internal factor in getting a loan approved is the credit reputation and presentation skills of the loan officer. Seniority always counts for a lot. Those officers who appear confident, speak well, and answer questions promptly and thoroughly do well by their customers in loan committee.

Why do you want to get your loan officer out to your place of business? So she can talk positively and personally about your company. So she sees in her mind your place of business when answering questions in the loan committee.

Why make sure the loan officer understands your industry? So she can respond with some personal insight or anecdotal evidence that is not in the credit department package.

Why go to bank receptions, meetings, or seminars? So the loan committee members will recognize your name and have a face and a favorable association to make with it. When selecting a bank, why do you care who is on the loan committee? Do you want a director who is a customer or a competitor of yours voting on your loan application?

Don't expect the banker to know a lot about your business. You will have to invest time and effort in getting the officer up to speed and in building a good overall relationship with the bank.

If you fail to educate him, you take the chance the loan officer will mistakenly overestimate the industry risks involved and underestimate the unique strengths of your company. These mistakes will not help get your loan approved.

Ideally your first visit with a banker should be through a referral from one of its solid customers. Bankers are trained to be suspicious of strangers. "Know your customer or borrower" is one of the first rules of banking.

You must send a signal to the banker that you are quite different from most business borrowers. You must show that you can make the officer's life a little easier and the loan application less troublesome.

Request a specific loan amount and describe in detail how you plan to invest the money in the business. Explain how your company will benefit from the productive use of the borrowed money. Use a projected cash flow statement to plan out a principal repayment program acceptable to both you and the bank. Protect yourself against the pressure of too short a repayment program.

Show the banker that the lasting earning power of your business, excess cash flow from profitable operations, will pay back the depositors' money.

Recognize that things can go wrong by supporting collateral values, by discussing the operating conditions of your industry, and by identifying optional business strategies.

Give the banker at least two complete sets of your entire proposal: one for the credit department to analyze and one for the officer's personal use. With her own copy the banker can work on your loan without having to remove your proposal from the credit department files.

The more your presentation can explain your industry and personalize your business, the better. Understanding the business also influences the perceived risk that assets pledged as collateral will lose their value or that business costs will become unmanageable.

The bank will order a personal credit report on you and on other signers or guarantors and on your business. Beat them to it. Review the reports before you submit your loan proposal. Correct any inaccuracies or file your permitted response to disputed or negative information.

If problems remain on your business credit report, prepare a brief explanation in the proper section of the loan proposal, usually when discussing suppliers and trade credit.

The loan officer's training says, "The past is a predictor of the future." All major operating decisions show up in the financial statements. Therefore, the lender will have a lot of questions about your past, current, and future financial statements and how you operate your company.

The bank does not assume you are honest and trustworthy. A lender will turn down your loan request if your personal or business history creates doubt that you can be trusted to pay your debts. In tough times would you place yourself or your business first?

What talents, skills, education, experience, ambition, drive, energy, commitment, and contacts will you bring to the business? Why will you survive when so many before you have quit or failed?

Make sure you can identify the Key Success Factors that make a business like yours profitable. What must be done day in and day out for your business to succeed?

Explain those local and national economic and industry conditions that influence your business. A banker sees risk in a business owner too tightly focused on the present and unaware of the external factors influencing the business.

Collateral is the traditional risk reducer to insure that depositors' dollars lent to your business are repaid. The more you increase the lender's opinion of the value of your collateral, the more you can borrow, the fewer restrictions might be placed on your company, and perhaps the lower your interest rate.

The business borrower must try to lower the risk-driven need for collateral and to increase the perceived loan value of the available collateral to the banker.

Capital is seen as a measure of the owner's commitment to the business. A loan decline because of not enough equity or capital in your company is almost impossible to overcome. You are likely to need a non-bank lender, such as a commercial finance company.

Banks do not like loose ends. You must thoroughly understand the financial statements yourself. Poorly presented and inconsistent historical financials create the suspicion that the business lacks financial controls and that management is unconcerned about the numbers.

A small loan request, without outstanding quality collateral and which requires a lot of restatement and analysis work can get turned down. It is simply not worth the effort involved.

Are you doing the lender's or credit analyst's work for him? I certainly hope so! The fewer questions and blanks you leave for the banker's negative imagination to fill in, the better off you will be.

It is your responsibility to come up with all the information, appendices, statements, and projections. Every time you cannot answer a question or have to go back for something else, every time you have to explain why numbers don't hang together or explain discrepancies and discontinuities, you lose points and look amateurish. Worse than that, you look like potential trouble.

When selecting a bank do not look only for convenience. Look for a bank with a reputation of serving your industry or your customers or your suppliers particularly well. A smart company tries to build a borrowing relationship, not just get a loan from any bank.

Do not pick a bank that is too small to handle your loans. All banks have a legal lending limit; the maximum amount the regulators allow that bank to lend to any one borrower. It doesn't matter how strong the borrower's financial position. This ceiling can be changed from time to time and it is different for national banks and for state banks.

Next, look for a locally owned bank with local businesspeople on its board of directors. They are more likely to be in tune with the needs of community businesses, can take a longer term view of loan policies, and can be more flexible within limits, but local banks see the same regulators that see the big banks.

You run the risk of less privacy as a small bank borrower. If the management of the bank is also its major owner, you risk having some arbitrary personal preferences and prejudices influence loan policies.

When you show up at the bank for your loan closing, never sign a bunch of papers you have never seen before, and leave with only a check or deposit ticket for the loan proceeds in your hands. You might regret it later on.

The way the bank presents the deal is not the way it always has to be. This is why your lawyer needs to see all the documents before you sign them.

Be sure you understand the terms and conditions that bind you and your company. Loan officers move around and bank loan policies change. The bank is bound to do only what is in the signed documents.

Some borrowers let the interest rate become a matter of ego. They want to borrow at prime. This is not a useful concern. The best way to lower your interest rate is to lower the bank's risk rating of your loan. Remember interest rates are negotiable. Establish with your banker that as you make your payments on time and as the bank becomes more comfortable with your company's performance, you expect the rate charged to move downward.

On committee-approved loans the interest rate is part of the loan officer's presentation. If you leave final agreement on the interest rate until the loan closing, you force the officer back into committee to get permission to make any changes. So if you don't like the interest offered at closing, the loan won't close. You take the chance of having the committee, given a second look, refuse your loan entirely.

Loan agreements with "positive" and "negative" covenants are becoming even more common. Test the covenants out against your business. Why are the covenants there? Understand the bank's true concerns and where they feel they need protection. Then draw up an agreement that fits your situation and meets the bank's concerns.

Never sign anything you do not clearly understand. Review all the documents ahead of time with your lawyer. Never rely on any verbal promises or statements. Recognize your borrowing needs in advance.

Plan your approach to the bank so you will have enough time to explore alternative sources and to negotiate terms and conditions.

The smart business owner begins preparing for the loan renewal or the next loan the day after the first loan is made. Borrowing should be a relationship, but today banks are treating it like a transaction.

The bank is under no obligation to renew your loan. If you don't have a pledge in writing to renew your loan, you have nothing. And banks very rarely give out such written agreements.

Don't take credit for granted. You should always be selling the bank on your company. Always tell the truth. Be open and honest. Nothing destroys trust faster than an uncovered lie, even a small one. Make only promises you intend to keep and keep all promises that you make.

Get your banker out to see your business at least once a year. Introduce the bookkeeper or accountant. Show off some of your methods like approving new credit, product quality controls, employee training programs and so on. Help your loan officer become an informed advocate for your business in the credit approval process.

Refer other high-quality businesses to your bank, but be careful. Someone you refer to the bank indirectly represents you. Don't refer weak companies and deadbeats.

Do not make housekeeping mistakes that cause your banker to lose confidence in you. Overdrawing your accounts, writing checks against uncollected funds, and making loan payments late are major mistakes that mark you as a sloppy businessperson.

Once confidence is lost, all is lost.

Successful borrowers know not to relax. They build a continuing relationship to assure renewal and availability of credit in the future. It is simply another task of management.

The banker may be friendly, but he or she is not your friend. Borrowing from a caretaker of deposits is a competitive situation in which both sides can try for a win-win conclusion.

Ultimately, the businessperson is responsible for the borrowing relationship and the banker is responsible for the lending relationship.

A FINAL THOUGHT OR TWO

I hope you have enjoyed reading this book. More importantly, I hope that it will contribute to the success of your business.

Please send me your comments. Tell me your experiences. Has the book helped you?

Let me know what you think of my ideas and suggestions. How can the book be improved?

Thanks.

George M. Dawson
P.O. Box 791283
San Antonio, Texas 78279

Special Appendix
Some Selected Tools

This appendix introduces and demonstrates several analytical tools or techniques used in credit analysis and in business management. The banker uses some of these tools to test the financial strength of your company. So should you, but before you visit the bank.

If you dislike dealing with the "numbers side" of your business, you will dislike this section also. Hang tough. Work through it one topic at a time. Have the "numbers person" in your company read it also. Discuss the concepts and decide which tools can help in your business.

Some of my number-crunching and bean-counting friends (credit analysts and accountants) say this section is too easy. However, the reality is that most of our businesses really need only good arithmetic and not high-order mathematics.

Some of the other tools are more specific to business management, but all can have an impact on the effectiveness of your loan proposal. You have a deeper and more lasting interest in your company than the banker. Consequently even non-borrowers should be familiar with and using many of these tools in the regular operation of their companies.

Accounting

Are you tired of feeling your bookkeeper knows more about the numbers than you do? Are you tired of only half understanding the accountant's jargon? A brief accounting review is in order. Most companies keep their books under a double-entry bookkeeping system. It is a method devised by a monk in Italy two years after Columbus discovered America. We have been tinkering with it ever since, but the essential principles are unchanged.

A balance sheet is a snapshot on one day of everything your company owns (assets) and how you paid for it (other peoples' money, also known as debt, plus the owners' money, known as capital and sometimes called equity). The balance sheet balances. The stated dollar value of your assets is equal to the sum of the stated dollar value of your debts plus the stated dollar value of your capital. And the double-entry system keeps them in balance.

Your income statement is more like a video tape. It is a summation of all income and expense transactions in your business over a period of time. It could be as little as a week or a month or a quarter, but rarely more than a year.

We keep track of all our transactions by writing into our books or journals what the good monk identified as entries. In fact we call them journal entries. Journal entries in the double-entry bookkeeping world have split personalities. They can either be a debit entry or a credit entry. (You will see credit abbreviated as cr, but debit abbreviated as dr. Maybe it is the Italian origin.) To keep things in balance, every credit entry must have an equal and offsetting or counterbalancing debit entry, and vice versa.

Journal entries can either make an account or item larger or make it smaller. If you pay cash for a new truck your cash asset account goes down and your truck asset account goes up. In the accounting world you would credit the cash account and debit the truck account. Now how did I know that? Easy! I have a system.

All items on the balance sheet are either what you own, ASSETS, or what you owe, LIABILITIES, or what has been invested, CAPITAL. All items on the income statement are either a form of INCOME or a form of EXPENSE. Rearrange the first letter of each of the five words and they spell the name A-L-I-C-E.

Now set up the following table. The plus sign indicates a journal entry which increases the account. A minus indicates the opposite. A debit to an asset account makes it larger. A credit to a liability account makes it larger. The reverse is true also. You pay a bill and your asset-cash goes down, a credit, and your liability-accounts payable goes down too, a debit.

Accounts	Debit	Credit
A	+	-
L	-	+
I	-	+
C	-	+
E	+	-

Connect all the plus signs with a line and you have what is traditionally called "Pregnant Alice." It's an automatic (if not the most tasteful) way to remember which half of a journal double entry is a Dr. or Cr.

Ratios

Ratios are important to the banker. There is only one consideration more important in the historical analysis of a loan request. That element is Character.

What exactly is a ratio and why is it important? A ratio is a numerical value calculated by dividing one number by another. Ratios can be written as numbers, dollars, or as percents. The ratios lenders use are financial ratios calculated from numbers taken from your income statement and your balance sheet.

The current ratio is one of a set of general financial ratios common to all companies and part of every credit analysis. It is a balance sheet ratio. It is the sum of current assets, those assets likely to turn to cash within one year (cash, accounts receivable, marketable securities, inventory), divided by the sum of the current liabilities, those debts that will have to be paid within one year (accounts payable, short-term notes and any long-term debt due in the same period).

Specific industries have developed additional sets of ratios that are unique to them. Ratios for automobile finance companies are very extensive and include such items as ratio of new to used cars financed, average term of loan, percent downpayment by new and used cars, percent of loans paying thirty days late, sixty days late, and so on.

Not all ratios are purely financial and are often expressed as a unit of output. Tracking labor costs per ton or raw material cost per ton in the steel industry or maintenance costs per mile in the trucking industry are examples of these industry-specific ratios.

Lastly some companies create and monitor ratios that are unique to the goals or structure of the company. Customer complaints as a percent of total sales, on-time deliveries as a percent of total deliveries, number of inquiries created by each ad dollar are examples of company-specific ratios.

What is the value of a ratio? A single ratio has no value. A group or set of ratios has value only if they can be compared or benchmarked to a similar set. Your company ratios are useful only when compared to other ratios.

Your ratios can be compared to other companies in your industry today and compared over time against the industry and against your own performance. Ratios provide information on where you are today and how you have been doing over time.

You can think of a ratio like a thermometer reading. You take your temperature and the thermometer shows 100 degrees. Is that good or bad? Do you have a fever or not? Are you sick or not? The "industry standard" or normal is 98.6 degrees. Even though "normal" for you might not be exactly 98.6, your body temperature is higher now than it is most of the time. In short, there is a reason for your 100-degree temperature. Is it a good reason? You are on vacation and sitting in a sauna. Is it a bad reason? You are in intensive care with pneumonia. What is the trend? Good, because your temperature is down from yesterday. Bad, because you are approaching heat exhaustion in the sauna.

The same approach applies to your business ratios. Your accounts receivable are taking on average sixty days to pay. Is it no problem, because you are a book publisher and these are common industry terms? Is it bad news because you are a wholesaler of men's clothing and your average has been climbing steadily from thirty days for the past twelve months?

Your receivables are paying in twelve days. Is it bad news, because you are a liquor wholesaler, where the industry average is seven days? Is it good news because you are an auto repair shop who has brought your receivables down from last quarter's twenty-two days?

Ratios are a tool to make comparisons, to identify trends, and to generate questions. How are you different from other companies in the industry? How are you different today from your own company last year and the year before that? What causes these differences? Is it a good difference or a bad difference?

Other books discuss ratios in depth. What follows is a basic introduction to the subject. The all-purpose financial ratios are grouped into five categories: liquidity, leverage, turnover, profitability, and trading.

The previously mentioned current ratio is a liquidity ratio, designed to measure your company's ability to pay its short-term debts. The quick ratio is a stricter current ratio, in that inventory is eliminated from the total of current assets.

The leverage ratios look at how much money you and other owners have committed to the business and how much your creditors and lenders have at risk with you. Divide total debt of the business, all the money owed, by real net worth to create this ratio. A debt-to-worth ratio of 3.1 says that for every $1.00 the owners have in the business, the creditors have $3.10.

Your ability to repay this leverage or debt is measured in at least two ways. Earnings before interest and taxes (EBIT) is divided by your annual interest cost. This ratio, times interest expense earned shows whether you might have too much debt in your company. If the ratio is one or less, your company appears risky and likely to have difficulty with your present creditors. Higher ratios show you could survive a sales and profitability slump and still keep your creditors from foreclosing.

A preferred ratio, often found in the credit department's analytical model, is cash flow before taxes divided by total debt service. This ratio adds depreciation to EBIT and divides by the sum of interest cost and required loan principal payments.

When figuring ratios that use numbers from the income statement, remember to first convert to a twelve month basis: multiply six-month data by two, quarterly data by four, and so forth.

Numbers from a balance sheet are as of a single business day and might not be representative of your normal operating levels of assets and liabilities. A good reason to prepare a balance sheet each month is so you can figure a yearly average accounts receivable, payables, and inventory to use in calculating the turnover ratios.

The turnover or activity ratios look at accounts receivable, accounts payable, and inventory. They measure on average how quickly your customers are paying you, how quickly you are paying your bills, and whether or not you are carrying too much or too little inventory.

Divide accounts receivable by credit sales and then multiply times 365 days. This gives the average number of days' sales held in accounts receivable.

Divide accounts payable by annual purchases and then multiply by 365 days. This shows on average how promptly you are paying your bills.

Inventory is divided by cost of goods sold and then multiplied by 365 days. This says how many days' sales you carry in inventory.

Some turnover equations use 360 instead of 365 days. It doesn't make much difference to the answer, but the major banking source of industry ratios uses 365 days.

The four profitability ratios look at different aspects of your profitability.

Three ratios use profit before taxes divided by either total assets or net worth or net sales. Are you using your assets efficiently? Are you providing a decent return to the shareholders? Are you bringing enough of the sales dollar down to the bottom line?

The fourth profitability ratio, gross profits divided by sales, looks at your pricing and manufacturing efficiency.

The two trading ratios relate to sales and are usually confirming ratios. They support conclusions drawn from the observation of the other four types of ratios.

Net sales divided by average net working capital shows how many dollars of sales are carried by each dollar of working capital. A declining ratio suggests a slowdown in customer receivables or a buildup in inventory.

Net sales divided by average total assets shows how many dollars of sales are generated by each dollar invested in assets. This ratio can be distorted by inflation and is not usually a significant component of most credit analysis.

If there are ratios specific to your industry, you need to know what they are. Be prepared to answer questions about how your ratios compare to the industry. Even better, answer the questions as part of your basic loan proposal.

Very large banks are likely to have an expert who knows your industry ratios. As a green credit trainee I popped off a complaint to my boss about having to calculate all those "stupid" auto finance company ratios. Three hours later I emerged from a numbing explanation of the value and nuances of each and every ratio.

Working Capital

This is a term used frequently and carelessly. The accounting definition is current liabilities subtracted from current assets. When borrowers say they need working capital, some need cash to pay bills created by the purchase of current assets. Other borrowers mean cash needed to cover operating losses.

In Chapter 10, I said a lender starts the review of your financial statements in the lower right hand corner of the income statement. Are you profitable? The lender can also do some fairly quick and dirty calculations using the turnover ratios. These calculations approximate how much equity or long-term debt your company needs to finance current assets and current operations.

Assume a company known for the rest of this chapter as Your Business or YB & Co., does $360,000 per year in sales. Cost of goods sold is $162,000 or 45 percent of sales. Accounts receivable are at $47,000, inventory at $15,750, and accounts payable at $14,850. YB's profits after taxes are 3 percent of sales or $10,800. Depreciation is $6,000 per year. Accounts Receivable Days (ARD) are 47 ($47,000/$360,000 x 365 days), Inventory Days (ID) are 35 ($15,750/$162,000 x 365 days), and Accounts Payable Days (APD) at 33 ($14,850/$162,000 x 365 days).

YB & Co. has, of course, more assets: cash of $10,000, equipment of $60,000, and more liabilities and capital: current bank debt of $6,000, term equipment loan of $20,000, and capital of $91,900.

If you add up Accounts Receivable Days and Inventory Days and subtract from this total Accounts Payable Days you arrive at the number of operating days requiring financing.

47 (ARD) +35 (ID) -33 (APD) = 49 Days

Then take your total sales and subtract your profits after taxes and also your depreciation. The remaining figure is annual operating cash. Divide this by 365 days to get daily cash.

$$(\$360,000-10,800-6,000)/365 = \$940.27$$

Multiply the daily cash times the Operating Days Requiring Financing. The resulting amount is YB's permanent or long-term working capital needs.

$$\$940.27 \times 49 = \$46,073.42$$

Permanent working capital? Yes! Ownership of accounts receivable and inventory in a going business is as much a permanent commitment as is ownership of land and buildings.

Permanent working capital should be paid for with invested capital or with profits kept in the business. It can also be financed with long-term debt and then repaid over time with excess cash from profitable operations.

It is rare to have a healthy business where Accounts Payable Days are greater than the sum of Accounts Receivable Days plus Inventory Days. It means the short-term creditors are financing the business. It most often means the short-term creditors are not getting paid on time and are quite unhappy. It means the business could not be liquidated and pay off its creditors. It looks like bankruptcy.

Too few borrowers understand that when they approach a lender to finance the payment of short-term bills or an increase in sales, they often need a longer-term loan. Seasonal buildups in accounts receivable and inventory obviously need a seasonal loan. Other loans that can be repaid by permanently shrinking inventory or accounts receivable or fixed assets are short-term also. Permanent growth requires permanent investment.

What if YB wins a new customer? Sales will go up $90,000 next year. How much permanent working capital might the company need?

Increase in daily sales is $90,000/365 days = $246.57/day. Required new permanent working capital is $246.57/day x (100% -3% Net Profit) x 49 Days = $11,719.47

How long will it take you to pay back this amount? If nothing else changes, less than a year. Current profits are $10,800, plus depreciation of $6,000, plus profits of $2,700 from the 25 percent annual increase in sales.

Now all the questions start. Can you handle an increase in sales of that size without additional equipment, facilities, or other operating costs? What if you are asking for only $5,000 for ninety days? What kind of first impression have you made on your lender?

Gap Analysis

Gap Analysis is another approach to the same subject. Calculate the percent of current annual sales ($360,000) of $47,000 in accounts receivable (13.0%), of $15,750 in inventory (4.4%), and of $14,850 in accounts payable (4.1%). Multiply these percentages times the new higher level of sales ($360,000 + 90,000) to get projected accounts receivable of $58,500, inventory of $19,710, and accounts payable of $18,450.

YB & Co.

	At Sales = $360,00	At Sales = $450,000	Change
Accounts Receivable	$47,000	$58,500	$11,500
Inventory	15,750	19,710	3,960
Accounts Payable	(14,850)	(18,450)	(3,600)
Financing Need	$47,900	$59,760	$11,860

You come up with the same number to be financed.

Now take a look at the whole balance sheet, before and after:

YB & Co.

	ASSETS			LIABILITIES	
	Old	New		Old	New
Cash	10,000	12,510	Bank Note	6,000	11,870
AcctRec	47,000	58,500	AcctPay	14,850	18,450
Invtry	15,750	19,710			
Current	_____	_____	Current	_____	_____
Assets	72,750	90,720	Liabil	20,850	30,320
Net			Term Loan	20,000	20,000
Equip	60,000	65,000	Equity	91,900	105,400
Total	_____	_____	Total	_____	_____
Assets	$132,750	$155,720	Liab/Eqty	$132,750	$155,720

What did I do? This is an extension of the assets as a percent of sales calculation holding cash equal to 2.78 percent of sales ($10,000/ $360,000). Those assets that change as sales change are called "variable assets." In YB & Co. variable assets total $90,720.

Also, YB & Co. knew it needed to add $11,000 in new equipment ($5,000 net after depreciation) to support higher sales. Equity increased $13,500 from the 3 percent after-tax profits on sales of $450,000.

Last, because these have balanced since the year 1494, I must "plug the gap" between the $22,970 increase in value of assets ($155,720 - $132,750) and the $17,100 increase in equity plus payables with new bank borrowings of $5,870.

What does this technique tell me as the owner of this business? It says:

1. assuming my operation grows 25% in sales over the next year, and

2. that this growth requires the same proportionate asset support as current sales, and

3. that the new sales will be as profitable as the current sales, then

4. I will still have to borrow at least $5,870.

Why "at least?" Because this approach summarizes the net effect of the year's operation. It is a static or rigid approach. It shows my year-end balance sheet snapshot. Might I need to borrow a larger amount sometime during the year? Absolutely maybe. It all depends on whether sales have a seasonal pattern, if the inventory purchasing schedule is uneven, if customers continue to pay in forty-seven days, and on and on and on.

Well, how do we handle all these potential variables and uncertainties? Not to beat a dead horse, but your best tool is a personal computer and a cash flow, income statement, and balance sheet projecting program. You can now evaluate the potential impact of seasonal variations in sales, schedule realistic inventory purchases, plan equipment down payments or installment payments, examine overtime versus second shift costs, and the like.

Sustainable Growth

The successful businessperson understands that an expanding business needs a growing base of assets. Growing assets must be purchased. Growing assets eat cash. They are "cash hogs." A profitable company or a product line whose growth has leveled off will be generating more cash than it consumes. It has switched from being a cash hog to a "cash cow."

Cash can come from only two places within the business, retained profits or selling off (downsizing) other assets. Or from two places outside the business: new debt or additional equity investment in the company.

Is there a limit to how much your company can grow? There certainly is. The limits are defined internally by your profitability and externally by your ability to carry debt or attract new capital. If your business is in a cash squeeze now, selling more of your product will most likely make the cash squeeze worse, not better. It is a rare company where the cash flow problem is not intensified by increased sales.

Think of it in another way. When the banker comes and puts you out of business, what do we call it? That's right, liquidation. Getting liquid cash in hand by stopping sales. If you cannot or choose not to borrow any more money or if you cannot entice new investors, then you can finance your growth only with your profits.

An excellent tool that extends Gap Analysis further was developed by Robert C. Higgins from the University of Washington. His equation can derive the annual percentage growth rate in sales that will allow your company to maintain its present debt-to-worth ratio, or to meet a new debt-to-worth ratio or to meet asset management efficiency targets. I like a variation of the equation to highlight variable assets and debt-to-worth:

Look again at our example, YB & Co.. The debt-to-worth ratio (D/W) is at .48 ($50,320/$105,400). Assume YB & Co. is also a risky business. So while you want to grow, you do not want your debt-to-worth ratio to get any higher than .48.

The equation looks like this:

$$\frac{\text{Net Profit as percent of Sales x } (1 + D/W)}{(\text{Variable Assets/Sales}) - (\text{Net Profit \% Sales x } (1 + D/W))} =$$

$$\frac{.03 \times 1.48}{(\$90,720/\$450,000) - (.03 \times 1.48)} = \frac{.0444}{.2016 - .0444} = 28.2\%$$

This says YB & Co. could increase sales each year about 28 percent and still maintain the target debt-to-worth ratio of .48.

That's not fast enough for you! The customers are beating down your door. So you go and talk to your local lender who agrees to keep lending you more money so long as your debt-to-worth ratio stays at .50. Great! How fast can sales grow now?

Back to the equation, but with two new features. We add to the top half of the equation the target "new" debt-to-worth ratio of .50 and an additional ratio called "present" net worth-to-sales ($105,400/$450,000). The bottom half of the equation also uses the target debt-to-worth ratio.

$$\frac{\text{Net Worth/Sales} \times \overset{\text{Target Today}}{(D/W - D/W)} + \overset{\text{Target}}{(NP\% \times (1 + D/W))}}{.2016 - (.03 \times 1.50)}$$

$$\frac{[(\$105,400/\$450,000 \times (.50 - .48)] + (.03 \times 1.50)}{.2016 - (.03 \times 1.50)} =$$

$$\frac{(.234 \times .02) + .045}{.1566} = 31.7\%$$

You could grow your sales at nearly 32 percent a year. As long as Your Business continues to keep all profits after taxes and the present financial relationships remains unchanged, the bank would continue to lend you money. Now that is pretty theoretical. As you know from reading this far, things change. At some point in time all that debt has to be repaid.

Now suppose your banker is no longer so agreeable. The debt-to-worth ratio has to remain at .48. Your product is a winner. The opportunity to grow faster than 28 percent is there. What can you do?

What if you had a smaller percent of your sales tied up in accounts receivable and in inventory? Think of it as planning your variable assets to be a smaller percentage of your sales.

You think you can reduce your accounts receivable down to 40 days, saving $7,000, and inventory days down to 25, saving $4,500. Now your variable assets as a percent of sales are ($90,720-$11,500)/$450,000 or 17.6%.

Go back to the first equation and put in .1760 instead of .2016.

$$\frac{.0444}{.1760 - .0444} = 33.7\%$$

Whatever you call it, managing assets more efficiently or increasing the turnover ratios or supporting a higher level of sales with the same amount of assets permits additional profitable sales growth. YB & Co. could grow annual sales almost 34 percent and still hold a .48 debt-to-worth ratio.

It is not likely your banker will run these equations. However, if you are negotiating a loan agreement with terms requiring a specific debt-to-worth ratio, the agreement is also limiting your sales growth. You need to know those limits and if you can live with them before, not after, you sign the deal.

Pareto's Law

Another handy device is Pareto's Law. Vilfredo Pareto was an Italian economist who died in 1923. He is given credit for identifying what is known today as the 20/80 rule. This rule says, roughly, that in a large population 20 percent of the inhabitants generate 80 percent of the activity.

As a non-economist banker I soon saw that 20 percent of my deposit customers held 80 percent of the dollars on deposit and that 20 percent of my borrowers accounted for 80 percent of the dollars borrowed. It became a quick way to sort out the important few from the trivial many. I saw that typically 20 percent of the customers of any business buy 80 percent of the product or services. Also 20 percent of the items held in inventory accounted for 80 percent of the dollar value of the inventory. Of your employee problems, 80 percent are caused by 20 percent of your employees.

No rule is perfect and sometimes it comes out closer to a 70/30 range. Policies can also distort the results. If we had an account that required a large dollar deposit to open, then the rule was not as accurate. The dollar balances were more evenly distributed among the accounts. Why? Because we had excluded smaller accounts from the population with the opening deposit hurdle.

The successful business understands this rule. In the loan presentation, recognize these key distributions in customers, inventory items, sales techniques, or advertising messages that have a significant impact on the company. Show how these items are being counted or controlled or managed or insured or rewarded.

Z-score

If bankers are not too familiar with the Higgin's sales growth equations, they are becoming more familiar with New York University's Professor Edward Altman's bankruptcy predictor, called a Z-score.

His statistical analysis of financial statements identified five financial ratios and measured the relative importance of each ratio to the financial stability of the company.

Look at YB & Co., whose stock does not trade publicly, with Altman's five calculations. Retained earnings are the after-tax profits kept in the business since it began. The pretax profits and interest expense are for the current period. Annualize these numbers if you are working these equations with less than twelve-month data.

Three additional pieces of information are needed. The equity of $105,400 is made up of $95,400 retained earnings and $10,000 original capital. Annual interest expense on the $11,870 bank note is $1,400 and on the term loan is $2,000. Pretax profits are $15,883 using a 15 percent tax rate.

1) $\dfrac{.07 \times (\text{Current Assets} - \text{Current Liabilities})}{\text{Total Assets}} = \dfrac{.07 \times \$60,400}{\$155,720} =$

2) $\dfrac{.8 \times \text{Retained Earnings}}{\text{Total Assets}} = \dfrac{.8 \times \$95,400}{\$155,720} =$

3) $\dfrac{3.1 \times (\text{Pretax Profits} + \text{Interest Expense})}{\text{Total Assets}} = \dfrac{3.1 \times \$19,283}{\$155,720}$

4) $\dfrac{.4 \times \text{Equity Book Value}}{\text{Total Liabilities}} = \dfrac{.4 \times \$105,400}{\$50,320} =$

5) $\dfrac{1.0 \times \text{Sales}}{\text{Total Assets}} = \dfrac{1 \times \$450,000}{\$155,720} =$

$$\begin{matrix} (1) & (2) & (3) & (4) & (5) \end{matrix}$$
Total = .0272 + .4901 + .3839 + .8378 + 2.8898 = 4.6288

This approach focuses on efficient use of assets and on present and historical profitability. According to Professor Altman's research a score of 1.23 or less says the company will be bankrupt within two years.

A Z-score between 1.23 and 2.90 is inconclusive. Additional analysis of the situation is needed. What is the trend of the Z-score for the past several years? What do the other financial ratios show? and so on.

Financially strong companies will produce a score over 2.90. With a Z-score of 4.6288, YB & Co. is in solid shape. Congratulations!

Depending on how weak your score is, you may simply be wasting your time looking for a bank loan. If your trend is in the wrong direction, you need to focus on getting more use or turnover out of the same amount of assets and on improving profits.

Break-even Analysis

Breaking even is not a lot of fun. However, this analytical tool gives some very useful insights that go beyond, "How much do I have to sell to pay all my bills?" It is easy to use and helps the business manager look at the relationship of prices, costs, and sales volume.

The previous financial ratios and tools were organized around the balance sheet. The break-even point is an income statement concept. Each of your expenses or costs will be one of three kinds: fixed, variable, or mixed. Fixed costs remain about the same over a fairly wide range of sales volumes. The property taxes on the land you own will not change if your sales increase substantially. Insurance premiums, equipment rental contracts, general plant maintenance, officer salaries, bookkeeping expenses, and legal retainers are usually fixed.

Variable costs will increase or decrease along with increases and decreases in sales levels. Sales commissions, packaging and delivery expenses, direct manufacturing labor, and direct materials are good examples.

Mixed costs are not so clear cut. Some part of your utility costs are fixed and some are variable. Supervisory costs might be mostly fixed, but could edge up with overtime work. Perhaps your salesmen are on salary plus commission.

You need to review all your mixed costs and divide them between fixed or variable. Then divide variable costs by net sales. After careful analysis YB & Co. identifies variable expenses of $236,733 which is 52.6 percent of the $450,000 annual sales.

So the first $.526 of every $1.00 in sales goes to pay for costs directly required to get that product into the customer's hands. Then there is $.474 left out of each $1.00 of sales to pay for the fixed or overhead costs. This 47.4 percent is called the "contribution margin." Each $1.00 of sales contributes this amount to pay for fixed costs. Since we know YB & Co. has pretax profits of $15,883, then the fixed costs must be $197,384 ($450,000 - $236,733 -$15,883 = $197,384).

How much do you have to sell to break even? The equation is:

$$\frac{\text{Fixed Costs}}{\text{Contribution Margin}} = \$416,486 \text{ Annual Sales}$$

A business manager can use the basic equation to think through the results of price and cost changes.

Let's add a little more information about YB & Co. The company is a manufacturer of high-quality lubricants for precision machine tools. Volume users buy the product in fifty gallon drums at $125 each. Each drum requires $65.75 (52.6 percent) in variable costs and makes a $59.25 (47.4 percent) contribution to fixed costs.

How many drums must be sold to break even? Divide fixed costs of $197,384 by the $59.25 per drum contribution for 3,332 drums. Or divide from the prior calculation $416,486 in break-even sales by $125 selling price per drum and you get 3,332 drums.

Your sales manager wants to drop prices to increase volume. She suggests $110 per drum. How many more drums do you have to sell to break even now? The drums still have the same variable cost, so dropping the price actually reduces the contribution from each drum to pay the fixed costs. The fixed costs are unchanged by the price cut. The contribution has dropped to $44.25 per drum ($110 - $65.75) or 40.23 percent of the new selling price (1 - 65.75/110).

The new break-even is $197,384/$44.25 = 4,461 drums, an additional volume of 1,129 drums. The required break-even dollar sales is $197,384/.4023 = $490,638. From a break-even perspective, a 12 percent price reduction ($15/$125) requires a 33.9 percent unit volume increase (1,129/3,332) just to stay where you were before the price cut.

Now you and the sales manager can talk realistically about who will buy all that new production. You also can decide if such a large volume increase will change any of your cost structures. Will your variable costs go down because you can purchase raw materials in larger quantities? Will your fixed costs go up because you need new filling machines?

Part of your variable costs is a 10 percent commission paid to the sales manager. You are thinking about raising it to 15 percent. Your selling price and all other costs will remain the same. This would raise your variable costs from 52.6 percent to 57.6 percent or $72.00 per drum. Your contribution margin has dropped to 42.4 percent or $53.00. The new breakeven is $465,528 or 3,724 drums. YB & Co. increased its variable costs 9.5 percent (.05/.526) and raised the break-even point by 11.8 percent.

Will the increase in income inspire your sales manager to sell more? Would you be better off setting the higher commission only on drums sold in excess of your 3,600 current volume?

Your bookkeeper needs a part-time assistant. Your fixed costs will go up $15,000 per year. You must sell 253 more drums ($15,000/$59.25) to cover the new fixed costs. A 7.6 percent increase in fixed cost ($15,000/$197,384) requires a 7.0 percent increase in drum sales volume (253/3,600) to pay for it.

How about raising prices to pay for the assistant bookkeeper? Using the contribution margin calls for an additional $31,645 in sales ($15,000/.474). This requires a price increase of $8.79 per drum ($31,645/3,600 drums) or 7 percent. ($8.79/$125). Will your customers buy from your competition rather than pay higher prices?

What would be your break-even if you raised prices $10 per drum and did not hire the assistant. The variable cost of $65.75 per drum would remain unchanged. The contribution margin would increase to $69.25 or from 47.4 percent to 51.3 percent [($59.25 + $10)/($125 +$10)].

Your break-even would drop to $384,764 ($197,384/.513) or 2,850 drums ($384,764/$135). You can lose 14.5 percent [(3,332-2,850)/3,332] of your present volume over an 8 percent price increase ($10/$125) and be no worse off. Another way to look at it is that if you lose less than 14 percent of your volume your company is more profitable.

What volume of sales would YB & Co. need to earn $50,000 before taxes? It would take $521,907 or 4,175 drums ([$197,384 Fixed Costs + $50,000]/47.4 percent Contribution).

Break-even analysis techniques allow you to convert changes in prices or costs into the realities of sales effort and customer behavior. Break-even is not the perfect tool. It does quickly provide dimensions and express relationships that can be discussed and evaluated. The analysis will be more complicated in a company with several different products, all with different contribution margins.

Break-even Debt Coverage

The banker has her own version of a break-even analysis. It is a measure of how much your sales could drop before you would be unable to make your loan payments.

You have to generate enough cash after paying your variable costs to pay your fixed costs plus your interest expense and your scheduled loan principal payments. This is a cash analysis approach. Depreciation is part of the calculation, and principal payments are made with after-tax cash. The equation is set up like this:

$$\text{Percent Sales Decline} = 1 - \left(\frac{(\text{Intrst} + \text{Fixd Cost} - \text{Deprecn}) + (\text{Principal}/(1 - \text{Tax Rate}))}{\text{Sales} \times \text{Contribution Margin}} \right)$$

Look at YB & Co. again. The only new information is that the bank wants you to pay the bank note off at $5,000 per year. Interest on the two loans is $3,400, fixed cost without interest are $193,984. Depreciation is $6,000, the tax rate is 15 percent, sales $450,000, and contribution margin 47.4 percent.

$$\text{Percent Sales Decline} = 1 - \left(\frac{(\$3,400 + \$193,984 - \$6,000 + (\$5,000/.85)}{\$450,000 \times .474} \right) = 7.51\%$$

If your sales drop more than 7.51 percent, you cannot make your pretax loan payments of $9,288 ($1,400 + $2,000 + $5,888). Is that right? Let's doublecheck.

Sales $450,000 x (1 - .0751)	=	$416,205
Less 52.6% Variable Costs		(218,933)
Less Fixed Costs		(193,984)
Plus Depreciation		6,000
Net Before Principle & Interest		$ 9,288

Cutting the principal repayment down to $2,500 per year increases the safety margin to an 8.9 percent sales decline. There is very little breathing room in the bank's request. Look at the historical pattern of your sales: have they ever dropped by 8 percent or more? This could be a very foolish proposal on the bank's part and even more foolish for you to agree.

More to the point, the preparation of a loan proposal must include this kind of an analysis. Again a good cash flow model will allow you to test out various sales projections and determine the sales level where the loan repayment program no longer works. This scenario might be worse than the "worst" case you have as part of your proposal.

As a matter of course, I would not recommend putting this particular analysis in your loan proposal. However, understand that a clever credit department is going to take a whack at this approach and then guesstimate how likely it is that your sales will drop to this point. If your banker asks for your breakdown of variable and fixed expenses, you know what is going on.

You should, if you truthfully can, eliminate concern about a sales drop in the historical narrative on your company. Show the upward trend in sales; comment that sales have never dropped more than a specific percent in any one year; stress the upside of your cash flow projections, and so on.

Ending Thoughts

Although this book is about how to acquire debt, debt itself is neither good nor bad. Too much or too little debt can be bad for your company. Too much debt raises risk. Too little debt can make you miss profitable opportunities. Some companies should borrow either very little or not at all. To make borrowing worthwhile, you must earn a rate of return on your assets higher than the interest cost of your loan.

Divide your Earnings Before Interest and Taxes (EBIT) by total assets to get return on assets. For YB & Co. this gives 12.4 percent ($19,288/$155,720). The interest cost is $1,400 on a note of $11,870 or 11.8 percent and $2,000 on a 10 percent term loan of $20,000.

YB & Co. is earning more on the loans than they are paying in interest. Interest rates do not have to increase very much to change this to negative. Could YB & Co. raise prices and keep the positive return on borrowed funds if interest rates go up?

On the positive side, YB & Co.'s management sees a conservative debt-to-worth ratio of 0.48 ($30,320 + $20,000)/$105,400) and a strong 2.99 current ratio. There is apparent satisfactory collateral coverage,

$65,000 in equipment (net) securing a $20,000 term loan and $58,500 in accounts receivable securing an $18,450 bank note. Further, the Z-score indicates no likelihood of near-term bankruptcy. The Higgins equations show YB & Co. could continue sales growth between 28 percent and 34 percent annually and still maintain satisfactory ratios.

On the negative side, their banker sees fixed costs moving up rather sharply as sales increase from $360,000 to $450,000. There seems to be no positive operating leverage because after-tax profits, as a percent of sales, remained unchanged at three percent. Only a modest 7.5 percent decline in sales will either endanger the loan repayment program or require reductions in fixed costs.

In a typical banking situation the lender will now begin to show some uneasiness and press for more information on the company, the collateral, industry, and the management. The borrower, who has done business with the bank for several years, feels the rules have been changed and becomes angry. The bank is standing in the way of YB & Co.'s growth and success. Rereading Chapters 8 through 10 will help point the way around this block.

Glossary

Acceleration clause is one of those items buried in the fine print. It has nothing to do with your car's performance and everything to do with your business performance. This clause should describe the causes or circumstances that allow the bank to call (demand that you pay) your loan before its scheduled maturity date. The bank declares the deal is off and wants to get paid in full.

A loan agreement can spell out in great detail which events can trigger the acceleration of your loan maturity date: fraud on your part, declaring bankruptcy, selling the company, or breaking specific loan covenants. If you have read the agreement ahead of time, understand the rules, and sign of your own free will, no problem. There is, however, often a "gotcha phrase" that says the bank can accelerate if it "otherwise deems itself insecure." This is too open-ended and vague. If at all possible, do not sign a note or loan agreement containing this phrase.

Aging is what happens to all of us. It is also what the banker wants to see for your accounts receivable and accounts payable. Agings are schedules of when all the bills and payments you owe come due and when all payments to you from your customers are due. When do you have to pay and when are you going to get paid? The bank considers these schedules essential to good business management. If you don't have them or do not keep them up to date you look like a real Bozo, and Bozos don't get loans.

Amortization means how many monthly payments it takes to pay your loan off completely. If it takes more months to pay off the loan than there are months in your note, then you have a balloon note. Your business can go pop when the balloon note comes due.

Assets are things that the business owns. They have been purchased either with ownership money (retained profits or direct investment) or with other people's money (loans and trade credit). Other people's money is also called liabilities. The accounting system says that what the business owns is equal to what was paid for it. Or assets = liabilities plus capital. This is known as the basic accounting equation (A=L+C) and must always be in balance. It reflects the underlying principle of double-entry bookkeeping.

Assets-Current are things the business owns that will convert into cash in the normal course of business sometime within the next twelve months. That doesn't mean that they will stay in cash form for very long, however. Your inventory will be sold, your customers will pay you and then you will immediately invest that cash back into more inventory or some other activity of your business.

So even though you could, in theory, find a buyer for your building within one year, the building is not a current asset because selling it is not the normal course of your business.

Assets-Fixed are things you own that can be touched, that will last for some time and are not sold directly to customers: land, buildings, vehicles, machinery, furniture, leasehold improvements, etc.

Assets-Intangible are assets that are neither current nor fixed assets. You could own patents, copyrights, or trade marks that have value. Goodwill is a special kind of intangible asset. It really has no value and does no one any good. It is created when a company is sold and the buyer pays more for the business than the assets are worth. It means either the buyer got taken or the accountants and lawyers were unable to raise the value of the assets to equal the selling price.

Balloon Payment is the last monthly payment on a loan and this payment is larger, much larger, than the normal monthly payment. I recently counseled a company that had borrowed $36,000 for five years at 16 percent. They paid $500 each month except the last payment which was $34,000. In the meantime, the lender had collapsed and the FDIC now owned the loan and guess what? They wanted to be paid and the company didn't have $34,000 lying about the shop.

Also real estate values had collapsed and the property originally used as collateral had fallen in value from $75,000 to $38,000.

A greedy and lazy lender made a 20-year loan on a 5-year note. An uninformed here-and-now business owner signed that note. A little less interest (14 percent), a little more downpayment ($5,000), a little longer term (7 years), a little larger monthly payment ($562) and the building would have been owned free and clear with the last payment.

Balance Sheet is one of the three essential financial statements needed to run a business. (What are the other two?) It shows, as of a single point in time, everything your company owns (assets) and how you paid for it all (liabilities and capital). Business owners are more interested in the income statement and neglect what the balance sheet can tell them. It is hard to put together a credible loan presentation without the last several years' balance sheets.

Belly Up is a term used to describe dead fish and dying companies.

Bozo is a foolish clown.

Break-even Point is that dollar amount of sales or number of units to be sold that will cover all your expenses and give you zero profit. The first sale after this point is your first profitable sale. You use fixed and variable costs in calculating your break-even point. While this sounds pretty theoretical, the Appendix shows some real-world uses of this type of sales volume analysis.

Capacity is what you, the business owner, bring to the table by way of business and personal skills, experience, attitudes, and abilities. Why will you succeed when the odds are that only four out of ten businesses will celebrate their fifth birthday? Just liking to eat is not sufficient capacity to run a restaurant.

Capital is what you don't have enough of or you wouldn't be reading this book about borrowing. It is the amount of money the owners of a business have committed to that business. It can be a sole ownership, partnership, corporation, limited partnership, etc. Someone other than the trade creditors and lenders must have something at risk in the business. Banks become quite uncomfortable when the owners' investment in the business is less than one dollar for every four dollars of other people's money.

Cash Flow Forecast is what you should tattoo in a prominent spot on your business. It is the single most useful financial tool for running a business and for winning the bank loan battle. It uses the unique cash flow patterns of your business to project when you might need to borrow, how much you will need, and when you can pay it back. It is a picture of the probable future.

Character is the number one factor in a loan decision. If the bank doesn't trust you, they shouldn't make the loan. Nearly thirty years ago a gray-haired loan officer told me that if the crooks wanted to get you, they could and that collateral had a way of not being there when you most needed it. Jerry was right then and the current financial industry mess shows he is still on target. So pay your bills on time, stay out of jail, and build a reputation in your community and industry for honest dealings.

Charge Off means a loan can no longer be considered as collectable. The bank can no longer pretend that the borrower will pay the loan. The bank must write the loan off its books by charging it to earnings or an earnings reserve. Banks hate this, but are required to do it by regulation or accounting rules. A charge off does not forgive the loan. The borrower still owes the money and the bank still intends to collect it. In fact, once the loan is charged off, the bank's attitude frequently gets tougher and meaner.

Christopher Columbus Manager is a business owner who doesn't know where he is going. When he gets there doesn't know where he is. Who, when he finds his way back home again, doesn't know where he's been and can't find his way back there again anyway. Only Kings and Queens are willing to make loans to him.

Collateral is the secondary source of repayment. It answers the banker's questions, "What do we do if something goes wrong? How do we get our depositors' money back?" If your business cannot generate enough excess cash flow from profitable operations to pay the loan, collateral can be taken and sold. Business assets, especially non-real estate assets, are hard for a bank to value. A key part of your loan proposal is in guiding the bank to assign the highest possible value to your collateral.

Compensating Balances is money that you leave at the bank in your account. You really could be using this money in your business, but the bank wants it on deposit so they can use it. This makes your loan more profitable to them. They earn more than just the interest paid on the loan; they earn on your deposit also. This is a better deal for the lender than the borrower. I have no idea why it is called "compensating." Have you injured the bank in any way by borrowing money from them?

Conditions are what is happening around you. No business operates in a vacuum. The woods are full of wolves, Red Riding Hood. What is good and or bad for your business? Who is your competition? What influences others to buy from you? What are the major risks in your business?

Costs-Fixed are those expenses of running your business that stay pretty steady regardless of whether your sales volume goes up or down: rent, property taxes, equipment lease payments. Obviously at some point these costs can change. You outgrow your building, you need more equipment, the tax rate changes; your insurance rating changes and so on.

Costs-Variable change as your sales change: sales commissions, direct piecework labor, shipping costs, raw materials, etc.

Covenants-Negative and Positive are spelled out in the loan agreement. They are not pacts with the devil, but they are the "dos and don'ts" of running the business that you must agree to follow if you want the loan. Covenants can cover any number of things: how much money you can take from the business, whether you can sell the business, if you can borrow money from another bank, buy other companies, and, indirectly, even how much you can increase your sales.

Cross Collateral Clauses are cross default's partner. They put all your collateral into one big pile pledged to that one big loan created by the cross default clause. Nifty, isn't it?

Cross Default Clauses are a banker's approach to togetherness. Cross default makes all of your loans at the same bank into one big loan. If you ever default on any one of them, you get a domino effect: If one is in default, they are all in default.

Deficiency Balance is a legal term meaning a world of hurt. You can't pay the loan. The bank takes over the collateral, sells it, and doesn't get enough to pay off the loan entirely. What your company still owes is the deficiency balance. This is why banks want personal guarantees on business loans. Now they can come after both you and your company for payment.

Float comes in two flavors: checkbook float and interbank deposit float. Neither is particularly good for you. Both can be dangerous to your business reputation and to the renewal, at maturity, of your loan.

First, let's discuss checkbook float. To pay a bill, you write a check and mail it off to your supplier. Now you know that check will not get back to your bank and come out of your account for several days. So even if you did subtract it from the balance in your checkbook, the money is still there at the bank. Well, what if there isn't enough money in your account?

That's okay, you say, because you will make a deposit and have the money in the bank before the check arrives. All well and good, except the collections you were planning on do not come in. The check hits the bank before the deposit and you have an overdraft. If you skipped Chapter 12 go read it now. Wait, "No problem," you say "That has never happened." Good, but suppose you are in Florida and the deposit you made to cover that incoming check includes a payment drawn on a bank in Elephant's Breath, Montana. Meet interbank deposit float. Your bank knows it will take several days for your customer's Montana check to get to its home bank. Your bank used to allow you to use the Montana dollars like they were Florida dollars. Now you have to wait. There is a scheduled availability for out-of-town checks.

So even if there is money in the bank and it is your money, you can't use it yet. Your funds are "uncollected." Which means that when the check you wrote gets to the bank, they bounce it. Now besides irritating the bank you have made your supplier mad. In fact, you lied to your supplier because your check promised payment, but you did not keep that promise.

Two or three service charges in a month for returned checks and you have lost any potential income you were seeking by being a shrewd money manager. Unless you are American Express (and if you are, why are you reading this book?), moving money around the world with full-time computer support, please follow Dawson's Cash Management Rule Number 1: Write no check before the money is in the bank. Dawson's Cash Management Rule Number 2 is read Rule Number 1 again.

Guarantor is the one who supplies the guarantee. The guarantor promises to pay someone else's debt if the borrower can't or won't. Most of the time, in a non-publicly traded company, the owners are asked to personally guarantee the company's loans.

There are a number of personal, financial, and emotional issues to be considered with guarantees. While it may not matter for most of us, special considerations can be created through divorce, remarriage, and community property laws. Get your lawyer's advice.

Holding Company Bank is a bank owned by a company that owns a bunch of other banks. Holding company bankers take orders from headquarters. Headquarters can be in another town or in another state or in another country. They can offer lots of services that many small businesses do not need and can lend very large amounts of money. They are not dependent upon the economic health of any one town or region. The holding company banker in your town may be only a cog in a machine.

Income Statement is one of the three essential financial statements. It shows how your business has done with sales, expenses, and profits over some selected time period. Both the balance sheet and the income statement are history. They have already happened. Accountants are historians.

Leverage refers to the relationship of debt to equity in a company. If you are using a lot of other people's money (OPM) as compared to owner's money to buy assets, then your business is said to be highly leveraged. "High" leverage varies from industry to industry, but if you have more than $4.00 of OPM for every dollar of your own, you are considered high. Banks are usually leveraged $10.00 to $1.00. For other people, banks consider high leverage to be risky business as interest expense and principal repayments wipe out the high-leverage company in business downturns. The highly leveraged company is often more profitable than a conservatively leveraged company in boom times.

Liabilities are money you have to pay others. It can be a formal loan or purchases you have made, but not yet paid for, or payments due in the future, like employee withholding taxes due next month. If you have to pay someone else, at some time in the future, then it is a liability.

Liabilities-Current are debts or obligations to pay others that must be paid, within the next twelve months, in the normal course of business. If you are making monthly payments on an equipment loan, the amount of principal that you will pay off in the next twelve payments is a current liability, even though the note may have several more years to run.

Liabilities-Long Term are debts and obligations that are not current liabilities.

Line of Credit-Seasonal is an agreement by the bank to lend no more than a specified dollar amount at one time to your company. This agreement is usually good for only one year. Often it is more of an understanding than a binding agreement, because not all banks will put it in writing. You should never enter into a line of credit agreement where you sign a note and the bank "talks" its end of the deal. Have your lawyer go over the note and the bank agreement with you before you sign.

A line is usually the most economical way to borrow. You are charged interest only for the amount of money you borrow, for the length of time that you use it. You borrow under the line when you need the money and pay it back when you don't. This in-and-out feature requires some paper shuffling and accounting by the bank each time you borrow or pay back. These administrative costs make small lines unpopular with many of the larger banks.

Sometimes banks want a "stand-by" fee. This is an interest charge, usually less than one-half percent of the total line, that must be paid whether or not you borrow. You are paying the bank a non-refundable deposit fee so that if you need the money, the bank will have it for you. It is a little like a room deposit.

Make sure you understand the conditions of the arrangement. Does the bank expect you to pay the loan off entirely sometime during the year? The bankers call this "resting the line." They want to be assured that the loan really is for seasonal purposes and that they aren't getting suckered into a long-term loan.

I was assigned a business borrower who had built a warehouse with a seasonal line of credit. She, an eighty-year-old lady, claimed the previous loan officer had never placed limits on the use of the line. I am pretty sure she was bluffing. I called and she refinanced the line at another bank. After that, my bank got real serious about putting lines of credit in writing.

If your company's financial condition has materially changed since the original deal was set up, the bank claims the right to refuse to advance money when you ask for it. The bank won't be forced into making the loan if your business starts losing money or developing other problems.

Lines of credit can be unsecured or secured, requiring that you put up collateral for the highest amount to be advanced under the line.

At one time there was a difference among banks about the meaning of a line of credit. Most banks said that if the line was for, say, $50,000, you could borrow and pay back up to $50,000 as many times as you wanted. A few others took the position that if you borrowed and paid back $20,000, then you only had $30,000 left for your use. In other words, your use of the line was cumulative. It is a small point perhaps, but review with your banker exactly how your line will work.

Line of Credit-Revolving is quite a different animal. Revolvers or "evergreens" usually require collateral and are for more than one year. Revolvers are made to companies whose accounts receivable and inventory are growing more rapidly than can be financed by company profits. These borrowers often have a seasonal or cyclical pattern to their sales.

Unlike the seasonal line, it is a rare revolver that is paid back down to zero during the year because the company keeps on growing. Revolvers are really a short-term solution to a company's shortage of equity capital. Revolvers are eventually paid off with a new long-term loan if the company's rate of growth can be slowed, or with new capital raised by the company.

Because the bank is hopping on the growing company's wagon with a "capital loan," revolving lines are approached with care. There are detailed loan agreements and a lot of administrative follow-up. Consequently, revolvers are usually large in size and available only to established companies.

Loan Agreement spells out the positive and negative covenants for your company's loan. It covers how the collateral will be valued, what kinds of reports you make to the bank, and how often you make them, along with a lot of other legal boilerplate, representations, warranties, and so on. Get a copy of the loan agreement before the loan closing. Review it with your attorney, and make sure you can live with it.

Loan Proposal is a detailed written request for financing which is presented to a bank or other lender. It takes a lot of work. Not many businesses do it well, if at all. It is one of the main tools to make your company stand out from all the others trying to get the lender's money. Please read Chapter 10.

Net Worth is another term for capital. Like capital it comes from either direct investment in the business by owners/partners/stockholders or reinvesting in the company by keeping after-tax profits in the company instead of paying yourself dividends or a big salary.

Overdraft. See float.

Ratios received a lot of discussion in this book. Trends over time and the comparison of one number's relationship to another number doesn't sound very exciting. But I don't think I over-emphasized them. The value of ratios as a tool for the ongoing management of your business is even clearer to me today, wearing my consultant's hat, than it was when I wore my banker's hat. Yes, there are many more than just the financial ratios. The capable business manager identifies these "other" ratios and educates the banker in their importance to the credit decision.

Risk is the four-letter word the banker sees in red on your forehead. A wide variety of real and imagined risk factors have been described. Your job as a well-prepared borrower is to be out in front of the banker, answering and diminishing these risk concerns before they can even be raised.

Robert Morris Associates was named after George Washington's banker. This organization, located at 1650 Market Place, Suite 2300, Philadelphia, PA 19103-7398, is probably the single best source of comparative financial ratios. They will sell their books and information to non-bankers.

SBA, The Small Business Administration, is a government agency whose second purpose in life is helping the smaller business. It has some really great low-cost publications on running a business, sponsors business information seminars, and provides valuable free advice and business problem counseling through the Service Corps of Retired Executives (SCORE). It can't lend much money itself, but does help and encourage banks and other lenders to make business loans by providing loan loss insurance.

Term Loan is any loan that is scheduled to be paid off in more than one year. The borrowing note has a maturity of more than one year. In reality, but not in accounting, any loan that needs more than one year to be repaid in full is a long-term loan. What's the point? You have heard it before. If you need two years to repay your loan, get a two-year note. Don't work with a note shorter than the needed repayment period. Those shorter notes keep maturing. You are dependent upon the willingness of the bank to renew or extend the note.

Banks like to have this exit window so they can make you pay off when they have changed policies or owners, need the money for something else, or have lost confidence in you.

Turndown is banker talk for "No." This book is about how to lower your chances of getting one. Unfortunately, it's a fact of life that not all of us can meet the requirements for bank credit. Many of my comments on handling a turndown are what I learned working with the finest loan officer I ever met. Ken voluntarily undertook the borrower "de-briefing," I describe in Chapter 13 whenever he declined a loan.

Working Capital is an accounting definition and does not exist in the real world. It is defined as current liabilities subtracted from current assets. As a concept it is really used more like a ratio for description, comparison, and analytical purposes. You don't go to the bank to borrow working capital. You go to borrow money so you can buy assets or pay for liabilities.

Bibliography

Behrens, Robert H. *Commercial Problem Loans*. Bankers Lending Series, 2nd ed. Boston: Bankers Publishing Company, 1983.

Bel Air, Roger. *How To Borrow Money from a Banker*. New York: American Management Association, 1988.

Bettinger, Cass. "What It Takes To Be A Professional Lender." *The Journal of Commercial Bank Lending* (March 1988): 4-10.

Boyadjian, Haig J. "The Scent of Failure and the Use of Risk Analysis." *The Journal of Commercial Bank Lending* (June 1989):43-50.

Brestoff, Nelson E. *How To Borrow Money Below Prime*. New York: Simon and Schuster, 1985.

Cook, John A. and Robert Wool. *All You Need To Know About Banks*. New York: Bantam Books, Inc., 1983.

Deloitte Haskins & Sells. *Financing Business Growth*. New York: Emerging Business Services Department, 1988.

Disman, Allan M., Robert E. Butler, and Donald Rapport. *Money and Your Business*. New York: The New York Institute of Finance, 1982.

Freimuth, Edmond P. *Turnaround: Avoid Bankruptcy and Revitalize Your Company*. Blue Ridge Summit, PA: TAB Books, 1989.

Goldstein, Arnold S. *The Complete Guide To Buying and Selling a Business*. New York: New American Library, 1984.

Hickson, Jennifer L. "The Quick and Dirty Details of Credit Software." *The Journal of Commercial Bank Lending* (March 1989):15-21.

Kemp, Robert S., Jr., and George A. Overstreet, Jr. "A Study of Information Needs of Commercial Loan Officers." *The Journal of Commercial Bank Lending* (February 1990): 47-57.

Kester, George W., Thomas W. Bixler, and Joseph M. Cheng. "A New Way to Evaluate Default Risk in Commercial Lending." *The Journal of Commercial Bank Lending* (August 1989): 4-9.

Krezanoski, Bryanz J. "Due Diligence in Middle Market Lending." *The Journal of Commercial Bank Lending* (July 1989):19-25.

McKinley, John E.,III, Ben F. Johnson, III, Edward P. Vollersten,III, R. Neal Batson, and John C. Weitnauer. *Problem Loan Strategies*. Philadelphia: Robert Morris Associates, 1985.

McNeil, Jane H. and Edward T. O'Leary. *Introduction to Commercial Lending*. Washington, D.C.: American Bankers Association,1983.

Milling, Bryan E. *Banking Strategies for Businesses*. Randor, PA: Chilton Book Company, 1987.

Morsman, Edgar M., Jr. *Effective Loan Management*. Philadelphia: Robert Morris Associates, 1982.

Omega, The Bank Training Company. *Commercial Loans to Business*. San Francisco, 1981.

Owen, Robert R., Daniel R. Garner, and Dennis S. Bunder. *The Arthur Young Guide to Financing for Growth*. New York: John Wiley & Sons, 1986.

Robert Morris Associates. *Annual Statement Studies*. Philadelphia, 1988, 1989.

Robert Morris Associates. *Credit Considerations*. Philadelphia,1986.

Schulman, Edward M. "Two Methods for a Quick Cash Flow Analysis." *The Journal of Commercial Bank Lending* (June 1988):29-36.

Sparks, Kenneth W. *Successful Business Borrowing*. New York: Walker Publishing Company, Inc., 1986.

Stancill, James McNeill. "When is There Cash in Cash Flow?" *Harvard Business Review,* March-April 1987, p. 38.

Index

Notes

Notes

Notes

Notes

Notes

Notes